JUMBLE®

JAMBOREE

Join
the
Puzzle
Party!

Henri Arnold, Bob Lee, and Mike Argirion

TRIUMPH
BOOKS
CHICAGO

This book is available in quantity at special discounts
for your group or organization.

For further information, contact:

Triumph Books
601 South LaSalle Street
Suite 500
Chicago, Illinois 60605
(312) 939-3330
FAX (312) 663-3557

Printed in the United States of America

ISBN 978-1-57243-696-1

CONTENTS

JUMBLE®

JAMBOREE

Classic Puzzles

JUMBLE®

Unscramble these four Jumbles, one letter to each square, to form four ordinary words.

HESOW

GAANP

URREBB

WOBETS

But I've looked everywhere

SUCH FRUIT IS NOT CONSIDERED MUCH GOOD WHEN UNOBTAINABLE.

Now arrange the circled letters to form the surprise answer, as suggested by the above cartoon.

Print answer here:

JUMBLE®

Unscramble these four Jumbles, one letter to each square, to form four ordinary words.

SULPH

WYDON

CINDIT

SILFOS

Hey! Did I ever tell you about that night in Vegas?

COULD BE ALL THAT FIGHTER EVER LICKED.

Now arrange the circled letters to form the surprise answer, as suggested by the above cartoon.

Print answer here:

JUMBLE®

Unscramble these four Jumbles, one letter to each square, to form four ordinary words.

BYBOH

OSSUE

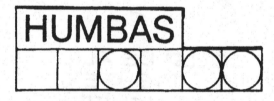

HUMBAS

FANNIT

An intellectual   That ain't all!

HE HAS SUCCEEDED IN BUSINESS BY BEING A MAN OF GREAT CULTIVATION—

Now arrange the circled letters to form the surprise answer, as suggested by the above cartoon.

Print answer here:

JUMBLE®

Unscramble these four Jumbles, one letter to each square, to form four ordinary words.

YIFFT

TOBOY

MILDIP

REEBOF

Hey! You're being chased!

SUCH A WARNING SOUNDS "POINTLESS."

Now arrange the circled letters to form the surprise answer, as suggested by the above cartoon.

Print answer here: A ⬡⬡⬡ – ⬡⬡⬡

JUMBLE®

Unscramble these four Jumbles, one letter to each square, to form four ordinary words.

NOPIA

STULY

COAMIS

GLERCY

I love you, too

SOUNDS LIKE A DRAMATIC LAST WORD.

Now arrange the circled letters to form the surprise answer, as suggested by the above cartoon.

Print answer here: " ⃝⃝⃝⃝⃝⃝⃝ "

JUMBLE®

Unscramble these four Jumbles, one letter to each square, to form four ordinary words.

AKELY

BELZA

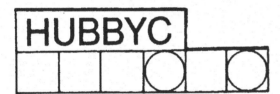

HUBBYC

COIPLE

USING THIS, A GOLFER SHOULD KEEP THE FIRST PART ON THE SECOND.

Now arrange the circled letters to form the surprise answer, as suggested by the above cartoon.

Print answer here:

JUMBLE®

Unscramble these four Jumbles, one letter to each
square, to form four ordinary words.

SYLOU

ASTEE

ILCAME

REHFIE

WHAT THE POTTER'S
ART CONSISTS OF.

Now arrange the circled letters to form the
surprise answer, as suggested by the above
cartoon.

*Print
answer
here:*  OF

JUMBLE

Unscramble these four Jumbles, one letter to each square, to form four ordinary words.

TRIHM

KARNC

SHERTH

RUFIAN

But, m'sieur, are you a Frenchman?

LES ELECTIONS

HIS "POSITION" IN *FRANCE* GIVES HIM THE RIGHT TO VOTE.

Now arrange the circled letters to form the surprise answer, as suggested by the above cartoon.

Print answer here: " ◯◯◯◯◯ - ◯◯◯ - ◯◯ "

JUMBLE®

Unscramble these four Jumbles, one letter to each square, to form four ordinary words.

CANKS

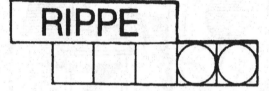

RIPPE

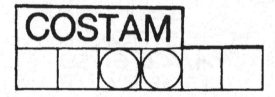

COSTAM

LINCEY

MORE COVER-UPS REVEALED

THEY HUSH UP REPORTS OF MURDERS.

Now arrange the circled letters to form the surprise answer, as suggested by the above cartoon.

Print answer here:

JUMBLE®

Unscramble these four Jumbles, one letter to each square, to form four ordinary words.

ALZEH

CLAWR

STOFFE

HOMARI

I don't want any guessing

ARITHMETIC QUIZ TODAY

WHEN YOU GIVE THE ANSWERS IN "ROUND" NUMBERS, YOU'RE APT TO COME UP WITH THIS.

Now arrange the circled letters to form the surprise answer, as suggested by the above cartoon.

Print answer here:

JUMBLE®

Unscramble these four Jumbles, one letter to each square, to form four ordinary words.

CELEX

NAPCI

PHEWEN

KANTLE

I'm in no hurry. Might as well enjoy myself

COULD IT BE A PLACE TO LIVE IF YOU'VE GOT TIME?

Now arrange the circled letters to form the surprise answer, as suggested by the above cartoon.

Print answer here: ☐ ☐☐☐☐

JUMBLE®

Unscramble these four Jumbles, one letter to each square, to form four ordinary words.

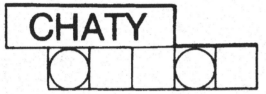

CHATY

ROPEA

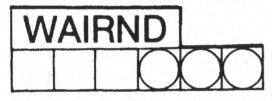

WAIRND

SILAAS

THIS MUSICAL COM-POSITION "INVOLVES" HARPS AT FIRST.

Now arrange the circled letters to form the surprise answer, as suggested by the above cartoon.

Print answer here:

JUMBLE®

Unscramble these four Jumbles, one letter to each square, to form four ordinary words.

GORAC

SCUFO

THOUPS

OTHPRY

WHAT THE ROOKIE G.I. WAS TOLD TO TAKE IN ORDER TO GET TO THE BARBER'S IN THE QUICKEST POSSIBLE WAY.

Now arrange the circled letters to form the surprise answer, as suggested by the above cartoon.

Print answer here: A ◯◯◯◯◯◯ ◯◯◯

JUMBLE®

Unscramble these four Jumbles, one letter to each square, to form four ordinary words.

BAXOR

YORFT

PLESIV

QUOPEA

COULD BE A SPORT "CONNECTED" WITH THE CLERGY.

Now arrange the circled letters to form the surprise answer, as suggested by the above cartoon.

Print answer here: " ◯◯◯◯◯◯ "

JUMBLE®

Unscramble these four Jumbles, one letter to each square, to form four ordinary words.

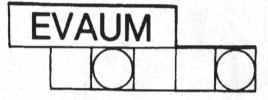

EVAUM

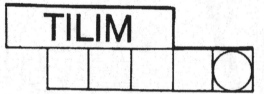

TILIM

WEEYAL

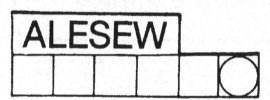

ALESEW

BANK

EVERYTHING IS "SOAKED" IN THE BILLFOLD.

Now arrange the circled letters to form the surprise answer, as suggested by the above cartoon.

Print answer here: " ◯ – ◯◯◯ – ◯◯ "

JUMBLE®

Unscramble these four Jumbles, one letter to each square, to form four ordinary words.

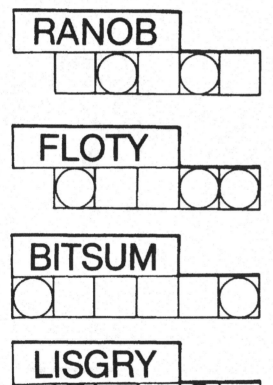

RANOB

FLOTY

BITSUM

LISGRY

WHAT "JACK AND THE BEANSTALK" IS.

Now arrange the circled letters to form the surprise answer, as suggested by the above cartoon.

Print answer here: A

JUMBLE®

Unscramble these four Jumbles, one letter to each square, to form four ordinary words.

YASTT

DROAR

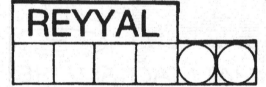
REYYAL

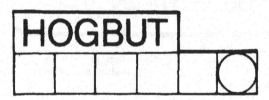
HOGBUT

But where's my check?

WHAT THEY PAID THE KING WHO WROTE A BOOK.

Now arrange the circled letters to form the surprise answer, as suggested by the above cartoon.

Print answer here: A ⬡⬡⬡⬡⬡⬡⬡

JUMBLE®

Unscramble these four Jumbles, one letter to each square, to form four ordinary words.

PLITO

LOGAT

VIEWLS

BRUHEC

Oh, she doesn't know me anymore

AN INSULT THAT SOMETIMES SEEMS RATHER SLIGHT.

Now arrange the circled letters to form the surprise answer, as suggested by the above cartoon.

Print answer here:

19

JUMBLE®

Unscramble these four Jumbles, one letter to each
square, to form four ordinary words.

UNREP

DULGI

BENRAY

CIANAM

WHAT YOU MIGHT
GET WHEN YOU
OVERLY INDULGE.

Now arrange the circled letters to form the
surprise answer, as suggested by the above
cartoon.

Print answer here:

JUMBLE®

Unscramble these four Jumbles, one letter to each square, to form four ordinary words.

VAHEY

YERFO

ALOONG

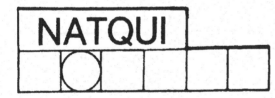

NATQUI

THIS SURE MADE HER FACE RED!

Now arrange the circled letters to form the surprise answer, as suggested by the above cartoon.

Print answer here:

JUMBLE®

Unscramble these four Jumbles, one letter to each square, to form four ordinary words.

FECOR

EUNEQ

SOUXED

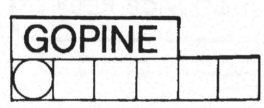

GOPINE

I AM THE FIRST ONE IN THE GRAMMAR CLASS

I DO WE DO
YOU DO THEY DO
HE, SHE, IT DOES

Now arrange the circled letters to form the surprise answer, as suggested by the above cartoon.

Print answer here: "  "

JUMBLE®

Unscramble these four Jumbles, one letter to each
square, to form four ordinary words.

ANCOP

YAWNT

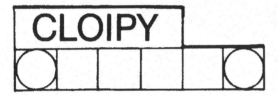
CLOIPY

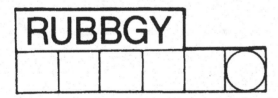
RUBBGY

MANY PEOPLE BUY
ON TIME, BUT
FEW DO THIS.

Now arrange the circled letters to form the
surprise answer, as suggested by the above
cartoon.

Print answer here:  THAT

JUMBLE®

Unscramble these four Jumbles, one letter to each square, to form four ordinary words.

TUPER

URSOE

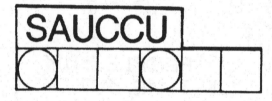

SAUCCU

JELIAD

You say it's on sale?

TAKE DOWN FOR A CUSTOMER.

Now arrange the circled letters to form the surprise answer, as suggested by the above cartoon.

Print answer here:
 THE

JUMBLE®

Unscramble these four Jumbles, one letter to each square, to form four ordinary words.

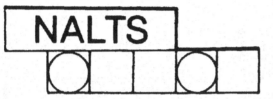

NALTS

SOGOE

PITTYS

REWESK

She looks nervous

WHAT THE ANXIETY-RIDDEN SOPRANO WAS EVIDENTLY SUFFERING FROM.

Now arrange the circled letters to form the surprise answer, as suggested by the above cartoon.

 Print answer here:

 " ◯◯◯◯ – ◯◯◯◯◯◯◯ "

JUMBLE®

Unscramble these four Jumbles, one letter to each square, to form four ordinary words.

NAYRE

OONNI

DOITUS

HYROTE

REWARD
TO
FINDER

WHAT HAPPENED
TO THE FARMER'S
CATTLE?

Now arrange the circled letters to form the surprise answer, as suggested by the above cartoon.

Print answer here:

JUMBLE®

JAMBOREE

Daily
Puzzles

JUMBLE®

Unscramble these four Jumbles, one letter to each square, to form four ordinary words.

MEHRY

NIGVY

SAUTLE

ENSTEW

THE CONSTITUTION GUARANTEES FREE SPEECH, BUT IT DOESN'T GUARANTEE THIS.

Now arrange the circled letters to form the surprise answer, as suggested by the above cartoon.

Print answer here:

JUMBLE.

Unscramble these four Jumbles, one letter to each square, to form four ordinary words.

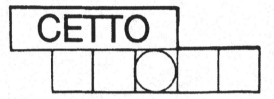

CETTO

RISUV

SUMMUE

LATBEL

They say it's a real love match

SHE MARRIED A BANKER BECAUSE HIS VIRTUES EXCEEDED THIS.

Now arrange the circled letters to form the surprise answer, as suggested by the above cartoon.

Print answer here: HIS "  "

JUMBLE®

Unscramble these four Jumbles, one letter to each square, to form four ordinary words.

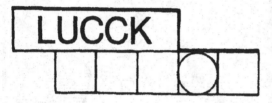

LUCCK

TAPAD

DILEEY

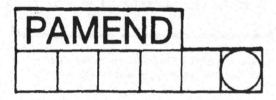

PAMEND

I smell sugar burning

Boss, you're terrific

SOME COMPLIMENTS ARE NOT SO MUCH CANDID AS THIS.

Now arrange the circled letters to form the surprise answer, as suggested by the above cartoon.

Print answer here: "  "

JUMBLE®

Unscramble these four Jumbles, one letter to each square, to form four ordinary words.

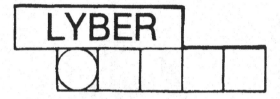

LYBER

YEDEK

TALKEN

DEGULC

Careful where you're driving

BANK

THE FIRST THING A MAN OFTEN RUNS INTO WITH A NEW CAR.

Now arrange the circled letters to form the surprise answer, as suggested by the above cartoon.

Print answer here:

JUMBLE®

Unscramble these four Jumbles, one letter to each square, to form four ordinary words.

OPUCE

PIGER

HATTOR

COIPLE

WHAT A SUCCESSFUL PICKPOCKET ALWAYS TRIES TO GET NEXT TO.

Now arrange the circled letters to form the surprise answer, as suggested by the above cartoon.

Print answer here: THE "⬡⬡⬡⬡⬡" ⬡⬡⬡⬡⬡⬡

JUMBLE®

Unscramble these four Jumbles, one letter to each square, to form four ordinary words.

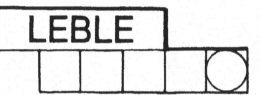

LEBLE

ROHTT

CAULNY

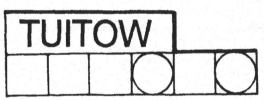

TUITOW

Closin' time

ALL-NIGHT CONVERSATIONS TEND TO BE DULLEST JUST BEFORE THIS.

Now arrange the circled letters to form the surprise answer, as suggested by the above cartoon.

Print answer here:

JUMBLE®

Unscramble these four Jumbles, one letter to each square, to form four ordinary words.

TOSOY

CLUHG

ARUSSE

LIVOAJ

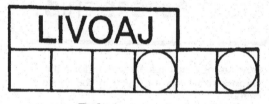

Since his last birthday there's nothing else on his mind

WHAT A BOY SCOUT BECOMES AT A CERTAIN AGE.

Now arrange the circled letters to form the surprise answer, as suggested by the above cartoon.

Print answer here: A ⭘⭘⭘⭘ " ⭘⭘⭘⭘⭘ "

34

JUMBLE®

Unscramble these four Jumbles, one letter to each square, to form four ordinary words.

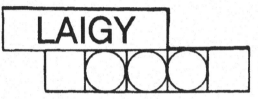

LAIGY

MIDIO

JELGUN

RIEVIL

HE WOULDN'T BE
IN SUCH A HURRY
IF HE KNEW HE
WAS THIS.

Now arrange the circled letters to form the surprise answer, as suggested by the above cartoon.

Print answer here:

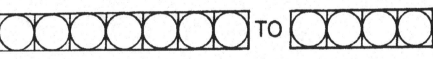 TO

JUMBLE®

Unscramble these four Jumbles, one letter to each square, to form four ordinary words.

NACHT

KLAYN

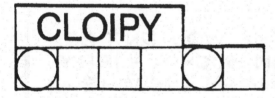
CLOIPY

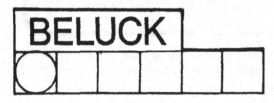
BELUCK

You sure charge enough!

For years I wasn't making a dime

WHAT THE CHIROPRACTOR'S FEES AMOUNTED TO.

Now arrange the circled letters to form the surprise answer, as suggested by the above cartoon.

Print answer here:

JUMBLE®

Unscramble these four Jumbles, one letter to each square, to form four ordinary words.

NITLE

SOSYM

REVONG

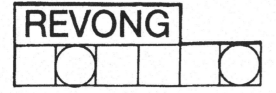

FIGNAC

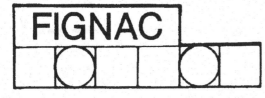

...And then I went to blah...blah...blah...

WHAT GOES ON AND ON AND HAS "ONESELF" IN THE MIDDLE?

Now arrange the circled letters to form the surprise answer, as suggested by the above cartoon.

Print answer here: ◯◯ "◯◯-◯-◯◯"

JUMBLE®

Unscramble these four Jumbles, one letter to each square, to form four ordinary words.

COPAH

YINNF

GLAHGE

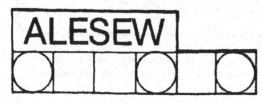

ALESEW

WHAT THE BALLPLAYER TURNED FARMER FOUND HIMSELF DOING.

Now arrange the circled letters to form the surprise answer, as suggested by the above cartoon.

Print answer here:

A " ⬡⬡⬡⬡ "

JUMBLE®

Unscramble these four Jumbles, one letter to each square, to form four ordinary words.

CROAH

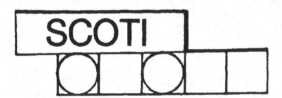

SCOTI

THELLA

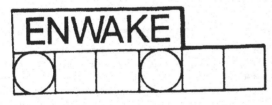

ENWAKE

Practically runs it all by himself

WHAT THE MAN IN CHARGE OF THE DOUGHNUT FACTORY SAID HE WAS.

Now arrange the circled letters to form the surprise answer, as suggested by the above cartoon.

Print answer here: THE "  "

JUMBLE®

Unscramble these four Jumbles, one letter to each square, to form four ordinary words.

NUBOD

CAUDT

LYMBAC

PERREF

ANOTHER THING YOU CAN'T TAKE WITH YOU.

Now arrange the circled letters to form the surprise answer, as suggested by the above cartoon.

Print answer here:

JUMBLE®

Unscramble these four Jumbles, one letter to each square, to form four ordinary words.

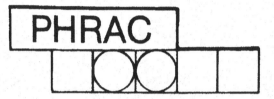

PHRAC

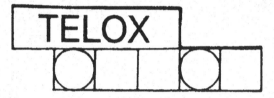

TELOX

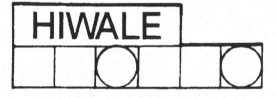

HIWALE

MELING

WHAT TUNE DID THE TEAKETTLE WHISTLE?

Now arrange the circled letters to form the surprise answer, as suggested by the above cartoon.

Print answer here:

 " ☐☐☐☐ ON THE ☐☐☐☐☐☐ "

JUMBLE®

Unscramble these four Jumbles, one letter to each
square, to form four ordinary words.

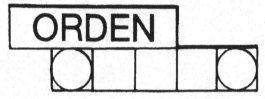

ORDEN

ERECK

KLEREN

DRAFTI

THE FEAR THAT
RELATIVES ARE
COMING TO STAY.

Now arrange the circled letters to form the
surprise answer, as suggested by the above
cartoon.

Print answer here: " ◯◯◯ ◯◯◯◯◯ "

JUMBLE®

Unscramble these four Jumbles, one letter to each
square, to form four ordinary words.

PORRI

LOGAT

VERYUP

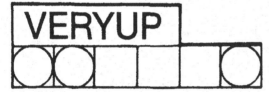

BURTAN

HE WAS SO LAZY
HE DIDN'T GIVE A
RAP, EVEN WHEN
THIS DID.

Now arrange the circled letters to form the
surprise answer, as suggested by the above
cartoon.

**Print
answer
here:**

43

JUMBLE®

Unscramble these four Jumbles, one letter to each square, to form four ordinary words.

LECCY

ADGUY

MAYLIF

EXLUDE

WHAT THAT MARRIAGE COUNSELOR WAS ALWAYS IN THE MIDDLE OF.

Now arrange the circled letters to form the surprise answer, as suggested by the above cartoon.

Print answer here:

JUMBLE®

Unscramble these four Jumbles, one letter to each square, to form four ordinary words.

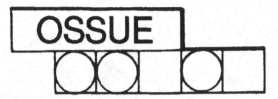

OSSUE

SYSAG

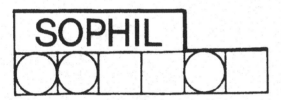

SOPHIL

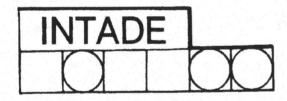

INTADE

FOR THAT FANATIC COLLECTOR, THIS WAS AN OBSESSION.

Now arrange the circled letters to form the surprise answer, as suggested by the above cartoon.

Print answer here:

JUMBLE®

Unscramble these four Jumbles, one letter to each
square, to form four ordinary words.

NELEK

MOAXI

DAHLER

RASTIE

HIS FOOTPRINTS
ON THE SANDS OF
TIME LEFT ONLY
THIS.

Now arrange the circled letters to form the
surprise answer, as suggested by the above
cartoon.

**Print
answer
here:** THE ☐☐☐☐☐☐ OF ☐☐☐☐

JUMBLE®

Unscramble these four Jumbles, one letter to each square, to form four ordinary words.

TCHAB

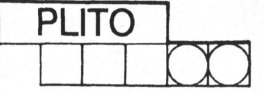

PLITO

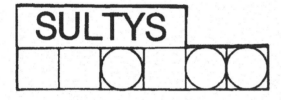

SULTYS

REHFIE

I'll never take a boat

SOME PEOPLE DON'T TRUST THE OCEAN, BECAUSE THEY'RE CONVINCED THERE'S SOMETHING ---

Now arrange the circled letters to form the surprise answer, as suggested by the above cartoon.

Print answer here: " ◯◯◯◯◯ " ◯◯◯◯◯ IT

JUMBLE®

Unscramble these four Jumbles, one letter to each square, to form four ordinary words.

VARNE

CEEPI

REEVER

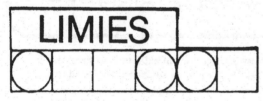

LIMIES

You'll be late for class

SOME MEMBERS OF THE RISING GEN-ERATION COULD RISE EVEN HIGHER IF THEY WOULD DO THIS.

Now arrange the circled letters to form the surprise answer, as suggested by the above cartoon.

Print answer here:

JUMBLE®

Unscramble these four Jumbles, one letter to each
square, to form four ordinary words.

RAYIF

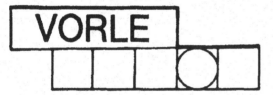

VORLE

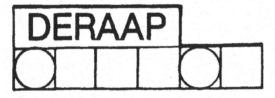

DERAAP

BIDITT

Say I'm not in

A DEADBEAT
STICKS TO HIS
FRIENDS UNTIL THIS.

Now arrange the circled letters to form the
surprise answer, as suggested by the above
cartoon.

Print
answer
here:

 " DO
THEM

JUMBLE®

Unscramble these four Jumbles, one letter to each square, to form four ordinary words.

TUXEL

STUMY

LYSEEP

VEEBAH

Road hog!

WHAT A CAR BRINGS OUT IN SOME MEN.

Now arrange the circled letters to form the surprise answer, as suggested by the above cartoon.

Print answer here:

JUMBLE®

Unscramble these four Jumbles, one letter to each
square, to form four ordinary words.

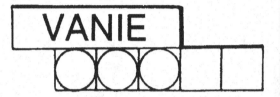
VANIE

INFEK

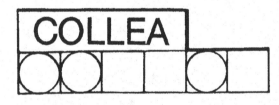
COLLEA

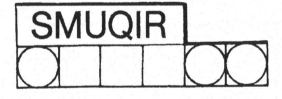
SMUQIR

HE BELIEVED IN
MARRYING A WOMAN
FOR HER FIGURE,
ESPECIALLY WHEN IT
DID THIS.

Now arrange the circled letters to form the
surprise answer, as suggested by the above
cartoon.

**Print
answer
here:**
 INTO

JUMBLE®

Unscramble these four Jumbles, one letter to each square, to form four ordinary words.

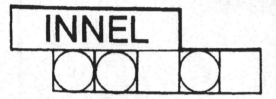

INNEL

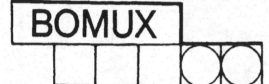

BOMUX

CRASAF

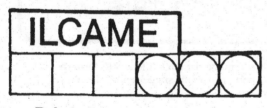

ILCAME

We're going to miss him

WHAT THEY EXPE-
RIENCED WHEN THE
LIFE OF THE PARTY
FINALLY WENT HOME.

Now arrange the circled letters to form the surprise answer, as suggested by the above cartoon.

Print answer here:

"   "

JUMBLE®

Unscramble these four Jumbles, one letter to each square, to form four ordinary words.

TCHEF

EUQUE

NOAZAM

CENNAD

Macs | Spy

FIT TO BE EATEN EXCEPT IN THIS.

Now arrange the circled letters to form the surprise answer, as suggested by the above cartoon.

Print answer here: ◯◯◯◯

JUMBLE®

Unscramble these four Jumbles, one letter to each square, to form four ordinary words.

FORVA

VOLCE

YIFTON

TIMOON

WHAT THE BIGAMIST TOOK.

Now arrange the circled letters to form the surprise answer, as suggested by the above cartoon.

Print answer here: ☐☐☐ ☐☐☐☐ ☐☐☐☐☐

JUMBLE®

Unscramble these four Jumbles, one letter to each square, to form four ordinary words.

FIDUL

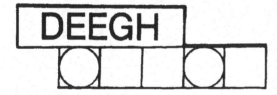

DEEGH

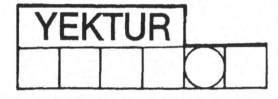

YEKTUR

TOIPLE

Boy—is he ugly!

WHAT POSITION DOES A MONSTER PLAY ON THE HOCKEY TEAM?

Now arrange the circled letters to form the surprise answer, as suggested by the above cartoon.

Print answer here:

JUMBLE®

Unscramble these four Jumbles, one letter to each
square, to form four ordinary words.

ETHAL

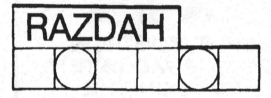

HALCK

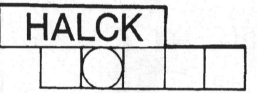

RAZDAH

WUNTAL

NEEDS TO KNOW
YOUR ZODIACAL
SIGN BEFORE SHE
TELLS YOU THIS.

Now arrange the circled letters to form the
surprise answer, as suggested by the above
cartoon.

*Print
answer
here:*
WHAT
YOU

TO

JUMBLE®

Unscramble these four Jumbles, one letter to each square, to form four ordinary words.

TAUCE

MEZIA

INZIAN

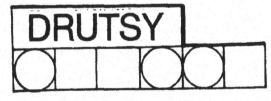

DRUTSY

THE FAVORITE FISH AT THAT OLD RUSSIAN COURT.

Now arrange the circled letters to form the surprise answer, as suggested by the above cartoon.

Print answer here:

JUMBLE®

Unscramble these four Jumbles, one letter to each square, to form four ordinary words.

NIMEC

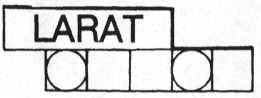

LARAT

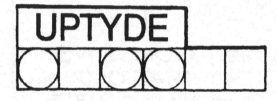

UPTYDE

ROOMAN

WHEN THE NEW FAVORITE ARRIVED AT THE ZOO, THERE WAS THIS AMONG THE KIDS.

Now arrange the circled letters to form the surprise answer, as suggested by the above cartoon.

Print answer here: " ◯◯◯◯◯ – ◯◯◯◯◯◯ "

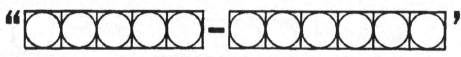

JUMBLE®

Unscramble these four Jumbles, one letter to each
square, to form four ordinary words.

WYLLO

HIWSS

AYGITE

TACHUG

A PIECE OF BEEF, AND MAKE IT LEAN

Now arrange the circled letters to form the
surprise answer, as suggested by the above
cartoon.

Print answer here: "⚪⚪⚪⚪⚪ ⚪⚪⚪?"

JUMBLE®

Unscramble these four Jumbles, one letter to each square, to form four ordinary words.

SNALT

UNHAM

QUIETY

GALUPE

Such cutting remarks are uncalled for

ANOTHER NAME FOR SARCASM.

Now arrange the circled letters to form the surprise answer, as suggested by the above cartoon.

Print answer here: "  "

JUMBLE®

Unscramble these four Jumbles, one letter to each square, to form four ordinary words.

ENSOO

RIPPE

NOOMIK

THRIME

Too expensive!

REPAIRS

Leave it to me

WHAT SHE THOUGHT SHE'D DO WHEN HER BOYFRIEND'S CAR NEEDED A NEW MUFFLER.

Now arrange the circled letters to form the surprise answer, as suggested by the above cartoon.

Print answer here:

JUMBLE®

Unscramble these four Jumbles, one letter to each square, to form four ordinary words.

INVEG

HERIK

FRUIPY

YEMMAH

WHAT THE MAN WHO INVENTED ROPE BUILT FOR HIMSELF.

Now arrange the circled letters to form the surprise answer, as suggested by the above cartoon.

Print answer here:

A ○○○○ "○○○○–○○○"

JUMBLE®

Unscramble these four Jumbles, one letter to each square, to form four ordinary words.

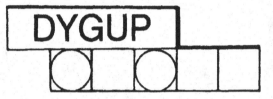

DYGUP

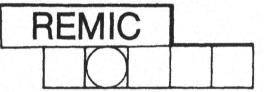

REMIC

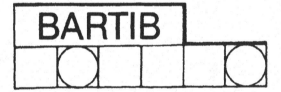

BARTIB

FINDEE

HAIR ON A MAN'S HEAD MIGHT BE PARTED WHEN IT'S NOT THIS.

Now arrange the circled letters to form the surprise answer, as suggested by the above cartoon.

Print answer here:

JUMBLE®

Unscramble these four Jumbles, one letter to each
square, to form four ordinary words.

VIALE

REMEB

DYNKIL

JURINE

HOW THE COAL
DIGGER'S FAVORITE
MUSIC WAS PLAYED.

Now arrange the circled letters to form the
surprise answer, as suggested by the above
cartoon.

Print answer here: IN A " ☐☐☐☐☐ " ☐☐☐

JUMBLE®

Unscramble these four Jumbles, one letter to each square, to form four ordinary words.

MYNEE

GOUCH

BALIVE

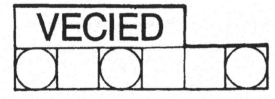

VECIED

WHY DRACULA DIED OF A BROKEN HEART.

Now arrange the circled letters to form the surprise answer, as suggested by the above cartoon.

Print answer here:

HE HAD  IN " ◯◯◯◯ "

65

JUMBLE®

Unscramble these four Jumbles, one letter to each square, to form four ordinary words.

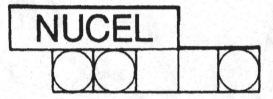

NUCEL

ABDEK

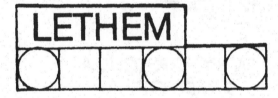

LETHEM

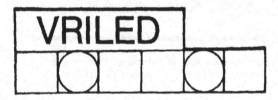

VRILED

Another one for my little black book

WHAT DON JUAN WAS.

Now arrange the circled letters to form the surprise answer, as suggested by the above cartoon.

Print answer here: A BIG "  "

66

JUMBLE®

Unscramble these four Jumbles, one letter to each square, to form four ordinary words.

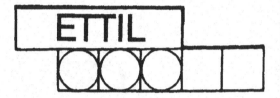

ETTIL

LUGAH

WROFUR

HUMILE

WHY HE ATE
SO MUCH BREAD.

Now arrange the circled letters to form the surprise answer, as suggested by the above cartoon.

Print answer here:

 HE WAS IN

JUMBLE®

Unscramble these four Jumbles, one letter to each
square, to form four ordinary words.

GUDOH

LODOF

ENVEAL

SMUTTO

A CONVERSATION
BETWEEN A TRAFFIC
COP AND A DRIVER.

Now arrange the circled letters to form the
surprise answer, as suggested by the above
cartoon.

Print answer here: A ◯◯◯◯◯◯◯◯◯◯

JUMBLE®

Unscramble these four Jumbles, one letter to each square, to form four ordinary words.

REMEG

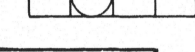
SYKAH

CADEED

FALLUW

It's about time he appreciated me!

WHEN YOU PAT A MAN ON THE BACK HE OFTEN ENDS UP WITH THIS.

Now arrange the circled letters to form the surprise answer, as suggested by the above cartoon.

Print answer here:

A

JUMBLE®

Unscramble these four Jumbles, one letter to each square, to form four ordinary words.

VALEE

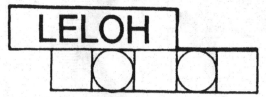

LELOH

BYSTUL

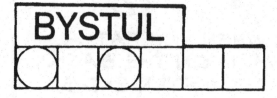

SUTTRY

She's been trying to trick us for a long time

WHAT THEY SAID IT WAS WHEN THAT RUSSIAN DANCER TURNED OUT TO BE A SPY.

Now arrange the circled letters to form the surprise answer, as suggested by the above cartoon.

Print answer here: A ⬡⬡⬡⬡⬡⬡⬡ " ⬡⬡⬡⬡ "

JUMBLE®

Unscramble these four Jumbles, one letter to each square, to form four ordinary words.

CANTE

YEEPA

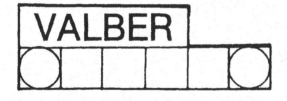

VALBER

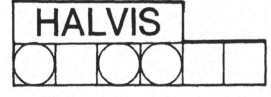

HALVIS

So nice to have him around

A WELCOME GUEST KNOWS WHEN TO DO THIS.

Now arrange the circled letters to form the surprise answer, as suggested by the above cartoon.

Print answer here:

"⬡⬡⬡⬡⬡ & LET ⬡⬡⬡⬡"

JUMBLE®

Unscramble these four Jumbles, one letter to each square, to form four ordinary words.

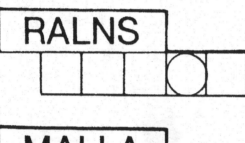

RALNS

MALLA

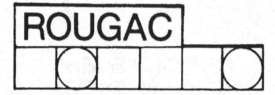

ROUGAC

INGROI

THAT EGOTISTICAL CYNIC SAW NOTHING GOOD IN THE WORLD, WITHOUT THE AID OF THIS.

Now arrange the circled letters to form the surprise answer, as suggested by the above cartoon.

Print answer here:

JUMBLE®

Unscramble these four Jumbles, one letter to each square, to form four ordinary words.

DITIO

ZUZYF

KORREB

NAITAT

...3...2...
1...GO!

WHAT AN ASTRONAUT
HAS TO BE BEFORE
HE REALLY STARTS
WORKING ON THE JOB.

Now arrange the circled letters to form the surprise answer, as suggested by the above cartoon.

Print answer here: "⬡⬡⬡⬡⬡"

JUMBLE®

Unscramble these four Jumbles, one letter to each square, to form four ordinary words.

PREKO

ESTAE

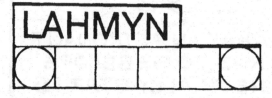

LAHMYN

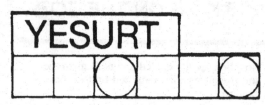

YESURT

This is fun!

WHAT THE GAME OF POLO INVOLVES A LOT OF.

Now arrange the circled letters to form the surprise answer, as suggested by the above cartoon.

Print answer here: "  "

74

JUMBLE®

Unscramble these four Jumbles, one letter to each square, to form four ordinary words.

NOICT

MULBA

TYKONT

HIGLES

WHY THEY CALL THEM "TELLERS" AT BANKS.

Now arrange the circled letters to form the surprise answer, as suggested by the above cartoon.

Print answer here:

 ALWAYS "  "

JUMBLE®

Unscramble these four Jumbles, one letter to each square, to form four ordinary words.

ENFLO

UCLID

RUSLAW

CHETOL

WHAT THE YOUNG COUPLE GOT WHEN THEY WENT TO THE MARRIAGE COUNSELOR.

Now arrange the circled letters to form the surprise answer, as suggested by the above cartoon.

Print answer here: A " ◯◯◯ – ◯◯◯◯◯◯◯ "

Unscramble these four Jumbles, one letter to each square, to form four ordinary words.

OTHIS

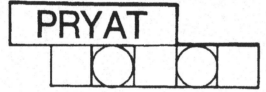

PRYAT

TOBUNT

CATHED

Good idea, Boss, but you're just wasting your time

HE AIMED TO PLEASE, BUT HE WAS THIS.

Now arrange the circled letters to form the surprise answer, as suggested by the above cartoon.

Print answer here:

JUMBLE®

Unscramble these four Jumbles, one letter to each
square, to form four ordinary words.

LISKY

NOROH

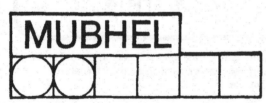

YORCAN

MUBHEL

IF YOU WANT
TO SUCCEED AS A
VIOLINIST, THIS IS
HOW YOU HAVE TO
GET INVOLVED
WITH YOUR MUSIC.

Now arrange the circled letters to form the
surprise answer, as suggested by the above
cartoon.

Print answer here: UP TO

JUMBLE®

Unscramble these four Jumbles, one letter to each
square, to form four ordinary words.

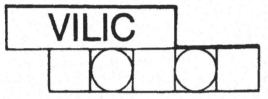

VILIC

ETHAB

GROUTH

HILERS

ANOTHER NAME FOR
WRITER'S CRAMP.

Now arrange the circled letters to form the
surprise answer, as suggested by the above
cartoon.

Print
answer
here:

Unscramble these four Jumbles, one letter to each square, to form four ordinary words.

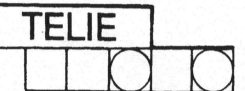

TELIE

NUNAL

FLYNUK

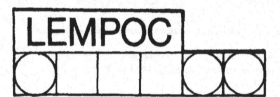

LEMPOC

Junior!

HOW HE GOT
THE JOB.

Now arrange the circled letters to form the surprise answer, as suggested by the above cartoon.

Print answer here:

 BY "  "

JUMBLE®

Unscramble these four Jumbles, one letter to each square, to form four ordinary words.

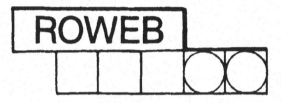

ROWEB

BEPOR

OPTATE

DILFED

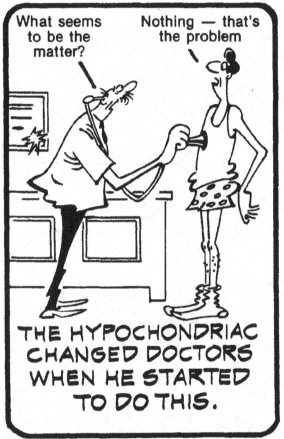

What seems to be the matter?

Nothing — that's the problem

THE HYPOCHONDRIAC CHANGED DOCTORS WHEN HE STARTED TO DO THIS.

Now arrange the circled letters to form the surprise answer, as suggested by the above cartoon.

Print answer here:

JUMBLE®

Unscramble these four Jumbles, one letter to each
square, to form four ordinary words.

DOORE

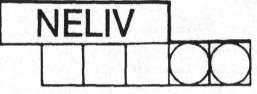

NELIV

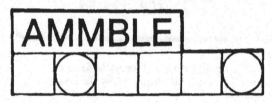

THYROW

AMMBLE

(Yawn)
I'll take
over, Dad

WHAT?!

$ $

HE OFFERED TO
HELP WITH THE
LAWN BECAUSE HE
NEEDED THIS.

Now arrange the circled letters to form the
surprise answer, as suggested by the above
cartoon.

*Print
answer
here:*

JUMBLE®

Unscramble these four Jumbles, one letter to each
square, to form four ordinary words.

CRIHB

HAWSS

PREDON

VALERM

A WOMAN WITHOUT
A HEART MIGHT
MAKE A FOOL OF A
MAN WITHOUT THIS.

Now arrange the circled letters to form the
surprise answer, as suggested by the above
cartoon.

Print answer here:

JUMBLE®

Unscramble these four Jumbles, one letter to each square, to form four ordinary words.

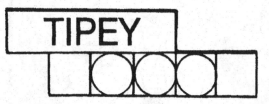

TIPEY

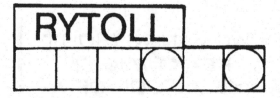

YICIL

RYTOLL

ALFFEB

Uh...er... uh...

HIS INABILITY TO TELL THE TRUTH TURNED OUT TO BE THIS FOR HIM.

Now arrange the circled letters to form the surprise answer, as suggested by the above cartoon.

Print answer here: A " ☐◯◯◯ – ◯◯◯◯◯◯◯ "

JUMBLE®

Unscramble these four Jumbles, one letter to each square, to form four ordinary words.

SPAWM

KIHCC

PRAULL

UPBRAL

VICE PRESIDENT

THE DOOR TO SUCCESS IS USUALLY OPEN TO PEOPLE WHO HAVE LOTS OF THIS.

Now arrange the circled letters to form the surprise answer, as suggested by the above cartoon.

Print answer here: ◯◯◯◯◯ & ◯◯◯◯

JUMBLE®

Unscramble these four Jumbles, one letter to each square, to form four ordinary words.

NAPOR

FECOR

POYNAC

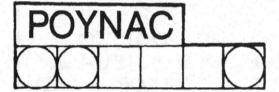

ELCHEK

WHAT THAT
ARROGANT INSECT
WAS.

Now arrange the circled letters to form the surprise answer, as suggested by the above cartoon.

Print answer here: A

JUMBLE®

Unscramble these four Jumbles, one letter to each
square, to form four ordinary words.

PUMIO

YIHFS

COSHUL

TIENNY

WHEN HE PROPOSED
THAT THEY GET
MARRIED, SHE TOLD
HIM THAT THE
OUTCOME WOULD
DEPEND ON THIS.

Now arrange the circled letters to form the
surprise answer, as suggested by the above
cartoon.

Print answer here:

JUMBLE®

Unscramble these four Jumbles, one letter to each square, to form four ordinary words.

TAYFF

NEYOH

GITHEY

ROCCUN

YOU SHOW POISE
WHEN YOU RAISE
YOUR EYEBROWS
INSTEAD OF THIS.

Now arrange the circled letters to form the surprise answer, as suggested by the above cartoon.

Print answer here:

JUMBLE®

Unscramble these four Jumbles, one letter to each
square, to form four ordinary words.

GEMAL

YORFT

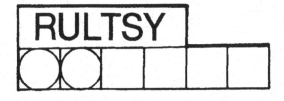

RULTSY

TUPPIL

IF YOUR "PANCAKE" MAKEUP ISN'T ALL YOU EXPECTED IT TO BE, YOU MIGHT TRY ADDING THIS.

Now arrange the circled letters to form the
surprise answer, as suggested by the above
cartoon.

Print answer here:

JUMBLE®

Unscramble these four Jumbles, one letter to each square, to form four ordinary words.

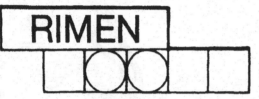

RIMEN

LANVA

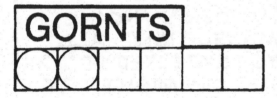

GORNTS

ROOLIE

THE RIGHT TIME TO BUY A BOAT.

Now arrange the circled letters to form the surprise answer, as suggested by the above cartoon.

Print answer here:

 WHEN THERE'S

JUMBLE®

Unscramble these four Jumbles, one letter to each square, to form four ordinary words.

GANOW

COKAL

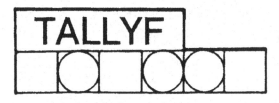

TALLYF

SURDIA

Wish I hadn't listened to my brother-in-law

You should have gone to a professional

THAT SO-CALLED FINANCIAL ADVISOR IS ALWAYS READY TO BACK HIS JUDGMENT WITH THIS.

Now arrange the circled letters to form the surprise answer, as suggested by the above cartoon.

Print answer here: YOUR

JUMBLE®

Unscramble these four Jumbles, one letter to each
square, to form four ordinary words.

NEFEC

TARFD

REPOPH

HERTHS

What a
surprise!

IF SOMEONE IS
NOW CELEBRATING
HIS BIRTHDAY,
THERE'S NO GIFT
LIKE THIS.

Now arrange the circled letters to form the
surprise answer, as suggested by the above
cartoon.

*Print
answer
here:* "   "

JUMBLE®

Unscramble these four Jumbles, one letter to each square, to form four ordinary words.

OPTIV

YOWND

TAYFUL

MOECEB

WHERE YOU MIGHT SEE A SHOOTING STAR.

Now arrange the circled letters to form the surprise answer, as suggested by the above cartoon.

Print answer here: IN A

JUMBLE®

Unscramble these four Jumbles, one letter to each square, to form four ordinary words.

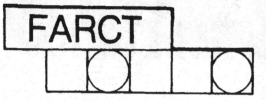

FARCT

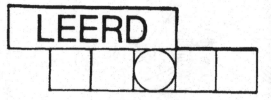

LEERD

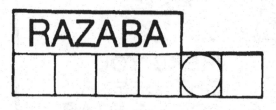

RAZABA

INFREY

WHAT HE SAID WHEN HE COULDN'T FIND A DECENT PAIR OF SOCKS IN HIS DRAWER.

Now arrange the circled letters to form the surprise answer, as suggested by the above cartoon.

Print answer here: "  "  !

JUMBLE®

Unscramble these four Jumbles, one letter to each square, to form four ordinary words.

TINJO

FORLO

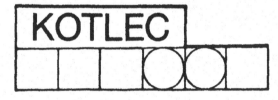

KOTLEC

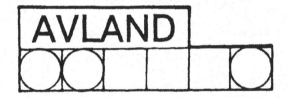

AVLAND

WHAT THE COACH KEPT SAYING TO THE TEAM OF ZOMBIES.

Now arrange the circled letters to form the surprise answer, as suggested by the above cartoon.

Print answer here:  !

JUMBLE®

Unscramble these four Jumbles, one letter to each square, to form four ordinary words.

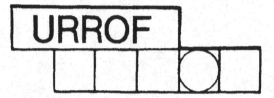

URROF

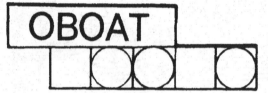

OBOAT

WADROC

TESKAB

Just as I thought

ANOTHER NAME FOR NEWLY HATCHED TERMITES.

Now arrange the circled letters to form the surprise answer, as suggested by the above cartoon.

Print answer here: "  IN THE  "

JUMBLE®

Unscramble these four Jumbles, one letter to each square, to form four ordinary words.

DUELE

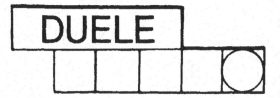

VENAH

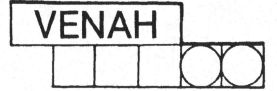

TUSDIP

NAUTER

Such grammar!

THE "TENSE" HE USED MOST FREQUENTLY WHEN MAKING SPEECHES.

Now arrange the circled letters to form the surprise answer, as suggested by the above cartoon.

Print answer here: " 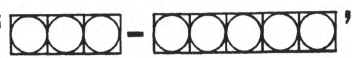 "

JUMBLE®

Unscramble these four Jumbles, one letter to each square, to form four ordinary words.

CEPEA

YADIL

FEWURC

KROMES

Now I understand why he's so successful

He's sure got brains

COULD THAT SMART COOKIE BE THIS?

Now arrange the circled letters to form the surprise answer, as suggested by the above cartoon.

Print answer here:

A ⬡⬡⬡⬡ " ⬡⬡⬡⬡⬡⬡⬡ "

JUMBLE®

Unscramble these four Jumbles, one letter to each square, to form four ordinary words.

PEINT

GITUL

TRAPIE

BIDROF

WHAT PEOPLE
SOMETIMES WERE
DURING THE
STONE AGE.

Now arrange the circled letters to form the surprise answer, as suggested by the above cartoon.

Print answer here: " 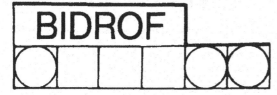 "

JUMBLE®

Unscramble these four Jumbles, one letter to each square, to form four ordinary words.

LUKKS

DRUIL

RYLAIF

GRENED

They're all too expensive.
Let's get out of here

WHAT SHE CALLED
HIM WHEN HE WENT
BACK ON HIS
PROMISE TO BUY
HER A MINK.

Now arrange the circled letters to form the surprise answer, as suggested by the above cartoon.

Print answer here:

JUMBLE®

Unscramble these four Jumbles, one letter to each square, to form four ordinary words.

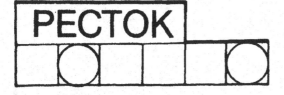

I think I dropped that information here

Careful!

MANY A MAN IS BURNED BY PICKING UP THIS.

Now arrange the circled letters to form the surprise answer, as suggested by the above cartoon.

Print answer here:

JUMBLE®

Unscramble these four Jumbles, one letter to each square, to form four ordinary words.

HICED

OAKEW

KEDONY

ATWIRE

We'll manage somehow

THAT CONCEITED GUY THINKS THAT IF HE HAD NEVER BEEN BORN, THE WORLD WOULD DO THIS.

Now arrange the circled letters to form the surprise answer, as suggested by the above cartoon.

Print answer here:

JUMBLE®

Unscramble these four Jumbles, one letter to each square, to form four ordinary words.

PARVO

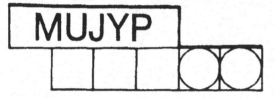

MUJYP

RUPPEA

LAYREY

Too young to get married

THE BEGINNING OF A DOG'S LIFE MIGHT START WHEN SOMEONE EXPERIENCES THIS.

Now arrange the circled letters to form the surprise answer, as suggested by the above cartoon.

Print answer here:

JUMBLE®

Unscramble these four Jumbles, one letter to each square, to form four ordinary words.

HARNC

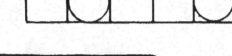

LAUFT

SHEARE

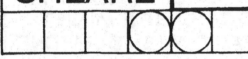

MILDIP

WHAT THAT PRECOCIOUSLY BRIGHT BABY WAS.

Now arrange the circled letters to form the surprise answer, as suggested by the above cartoon.

Print answer here: A  IN THE "  "

JUMBLE®

Unscramble these four Jumbles, one letter to each square, to form four ordinary words.

ODITI

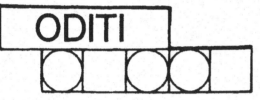

UNDOB

CHEPSY

HOMAFT

Some of them just made it by a hair

WHAT THAT GRADUATION PICTURE WAS.

Now arrange the circled letters to form the surprise answer, as suggested by the above cartoon.

Print answer here: A

JUMBLE®

Unscramble these four Jumbles, one letter to each square, to form four ordinary words.

WATHE

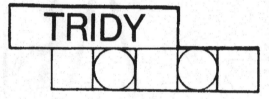

TRIDY

EMTYSS

SILFOS

I'm not sure he's ready yet

SHOULD A CAR WITH AUTOMATIC DRIVE BE ENTRUSTED TO SOME-ONE WHO'S THIS?

Now arrange the circled letters to form the surprise answer, as suggested by the above cartoon.

Print answer here: " ◯◯◯◯◯◯◯◯◯ "

JUMBLE®

Unscramble these four Jumbles, one letter to each square, to form four ordinary words.

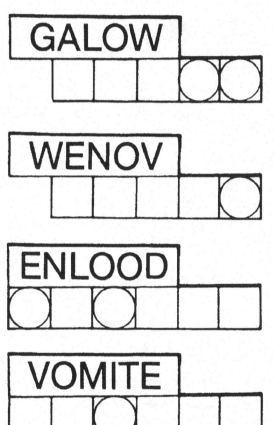

GALOW

WENOV

ENLOOD

VOMITE

WHEN THEY GAVE THAT HUGE BANQUET IN CHINA, HOW MUCH DID THE FOOD WEIGH?

Now arrange the circled letters to form the surprise answer, as suggested by the above cartoon.

Print answer here: "  "

JUMBLE®

Unscramble these four Jumbles, one letter to each
square, to form four ordinary words.

HESAF

LUTOC

EMBLUF

YARTTE

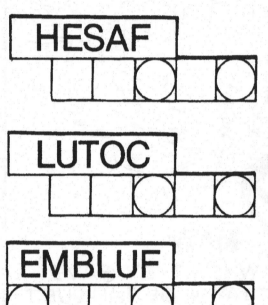

I'm just fine, but I don't
want any more of that beast

HORSEBACK RIDING
IS A SPORT THAT
SOMETIMES MAKES THE
NOVICE FEEL THIS.

Now arrange the circled letters to form the
surprise answer, as suggested by the above
cartoon.

Print answer here:

108

JUMBLE®

Unscramble these four Jumbles, one letter to each square, to form four ordinary words.

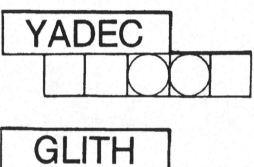

YADEC

GLITH

CYMALL

YARBEK

Someone is going to have to pay for this

WHAT THERE WAS PLENTY OF AFTER THE POST OFFICE CAUGHT FIRE.

Now arrange the circled letters to form the surprise answer, as suggested by the above cartoon.

Print answer here: " ◯◯◯◯◯ ◯◯◯◯ "

JUMBLE.

Unscramble these four Jumbles, one letter to each square, to form four ordinary words.

EUQER

NAFTI

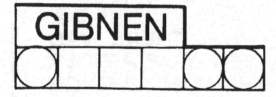

GIBNEN

TARNEK

Come along now

INVESTMENTS

HE THINKS HE'S GOING PLACES WHEN HE'S REALLY THIS.

Now arrange the circled letters to form the surprise answer, as suggested by the above cartoon.

Print answer here:

 "  "

JUMBLE®

Unscramble these four Jumbles, one letter to each
square, to form four ordinary words.

DARUG

THICH

SCYTIK

CYSTOL

SALES
OFFICE

WHAT TO SAY TO THE
MAN WHO THINKS HE
CAN AFFORD A
BOAT LIKE THAT.

Now arrange the circled letters to form the
surprise answer, as suggested by the above
cartoon.

*Print
answer
here:*

JUMBLE®

Unscramble these four Jumbles, one letter to each square, to form four ordinary words.

CRAID

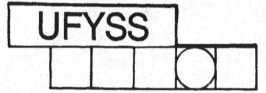

UFYSS

LARTEY

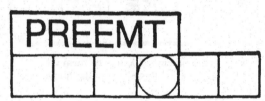

PREEMT

NASA PERSONNEL OFFICE

HE WANTED TO BE AN ASTRONAUT, BUT THEY SAID ALL HE HAD TAKEN UP IN SCHOOL WAS THIS.

Now arrange the circled letters to form the surprise answer, as suggested by the above cartoon.

Print answer here: " ⬡⬡⬡⬡⬡ "

JUMBLE®

Unscramble these four Jumbles, one letter to each square, to form four ordinary words.

NOPIA

PUTIL

TUILGY

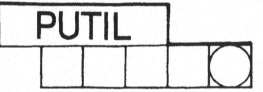

UPDINT

Aren't you supposed to be watching what you eat?

A DIET IS SOME-THING YOU KEEP PUTTING OFF WHILE YOU KEEP THIS.

Now arrange the circled letters to form the surprise answer, as suggested by the above cartoon.

Print answer here:

JUMBLE®

Unscramble these four Jumbles, one letter to each square, to form four ordinary words.

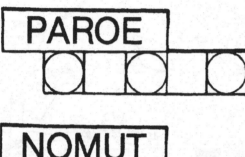

PAROE

NOMUT

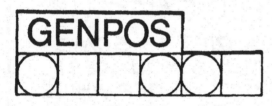

GENPOS

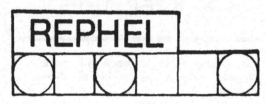

REPHEL

WHAT THAT TALL BEACHCOMBER WAS.

Now arrange the circled letters to form the surprise answer, as suggested by the above cartoon.

Print answer A here:

JUMBLE®

Unscramble these four Jumbles, one letter to each square, to form four ordinary words.

INGIC

LUGIE

SNIULF

MARLOF

I worked my head off today, but I made us a lot of money

PEOPLE WHO GO ALL OUT OFTEN END UP THIS WAY.

Now arrange the circled letters to form the surprise answer, as suggested by the above cartoon.

Print answer here:

JUMBLE®

Unscramble these four Jumbles, one letter to each square, to form four ordinary words.

HURCS

PUPER

RECUPS

YORPOL

I'm down here, Harold

AN ELOPEMENT SOMETIMES RESULTS WHEN MAN PROPOSES AND FUTURE MOTHER-IN-LAW DOES THIS.

Now arrange the circled letters to form the surprise answer, as suggested by the above cartoon.

Print answer here:

JUMBLE®

Unscramble these four Jumbles, one letter to each square, to form four ordinary words.

TROIB

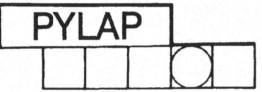

PYLAP

CHERAG

YAMBIG

CANDLES ON
BIRTHDAY CAKES
HELP PEOPLE
MAKE THIS.

Now arrange the circled letters to form the surprise answer, as suggested by the above cartoon.

Print answer here: "  " OF THEIR

JUMBLE®

Unscramble these four Jumbles, one letter to each square, to form four ordinary words.

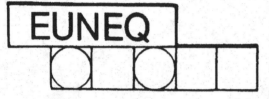

EUNEQ

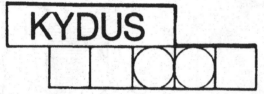

KYDUS

TARBUL

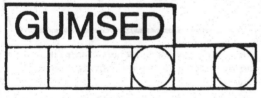

GUMSED

HOW AUTOMOBILES MOVED BEFORE ANY-ONE THOUGHT OF USING LUBRICATING OIL.

Now arrange the circled letters to form the surprise answer, as suggested by the above cartoon.

Print answer here:

THEY JUST ⬡⬡⬡⬡⬡⬡⬡⬡⬡⬡ BY

JUMBLE®

Unscramble these four Jumbles, one letter to each
square, to form four ordinary words.

KNALF

EVVAL

THARRE

YABSUW

WHAT'S THE ENVI-
RONMENT LIKE WHEN
YOU SLEEP ALONG-
SIDE YOUR HORSE?

Now arrange the circled letters to form the
surprise answer, as suggested by the above
cartoon.

Print answer here:

JUMBLE®

Unscramble these four Jumbles, one letter to each square, to form four ordinary words.

ENCAP

DRUGO

RUNUTE

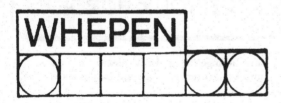

WHEPEN

I'm not surprised

CLOSED

WHAT HAPPENED TO THE RESTAURANT THAT SERVED THOSE SUBSTANDARD SUB-MARINE SANDWICHES?

Now arrange the circled letters to form the surprise answer, as suggested by the above cartoon.

Print answer here: IT

JUMBLE®

Unscramble these four Jumbles, one letter to each
square, to form four ordinary words.

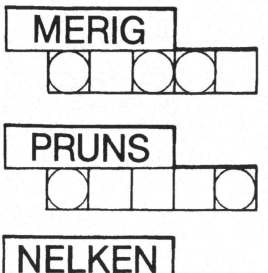

MERIG

PRUNS

NELKEN

TINISS

WHAT THE COPS
LOOKED FOR WHEN
THERE WAS A
ROBBERY AT THE
SAUSAGE FACTORY.

Now arrange the circled letters to form the
surprise answer, as suggested by the above
cartoon.

**Print
answer
here:** THE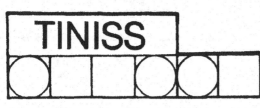

121

JUMBLE®

Unscramble these four Jumbles, one letter to each square, to form four ordinary words.

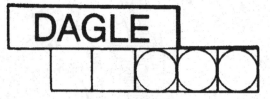

DAGLE

TARAP

OKOCIE

HOGUNE

WHAT THOSE STRAY DOGS ENJOYED MOST AT DINNERTIME.

Now arrange the circled letters to form the surprise answer, as suggested by the above cartoon.

Print answer here: " ⬚⬚⬚⬚⬚ " ⬚⬚⬚⬚

JUMBLE®

Unscramble these four Jumbles, one letter to each
square, to form four ordinary words.

BECAL

PUROG

AMBALS

SNUFUG

WHAT THAT
HEROIC FIREMAN
BECAME.

Now arrange the circled letters to form the
surprise answer, as suggested by the above
cartoon.

Print answer here: " ⭘⭘⭘⭘⭘⭘⭘ "

JUMBLE®

Unscramble these four Jumbles, one letter to each square, to form four ordinary words.

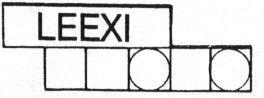

LEEXI

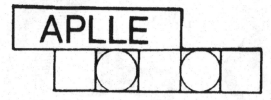

APLLE

INPROS

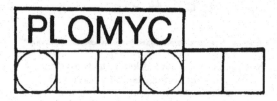

PLOMYC

WHAT YOU MIGHT FIND AT THAT MOM AND POP TIRE SHOP.

Now arrange the circled letters to form the surprise answer, as suggested by the above cartoon.

Print answer here:

A  "  "

JUMBLE®

Unscramble these four Jumbles, one letter to each square, to form four ordinary words.

NONAY

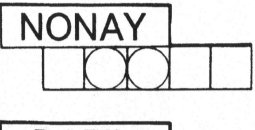

DAPIL

LAPLOW

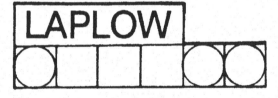

INTEWG

Dear, why don't you get someone to help you?

WHAT YOU MIGHT END UP WITH FROM TOO MUCH HOUSE-CLEANING.

Now arrange the circled letters to form the surprise answer, as suggested by the above cartoon.

Print answer here: A ◯◯◯◯◯◯ " ◯◯◯◯ "

JUMBLE®

Unscramble these four Jumbles, one letter to each square, to form four ordinary words.

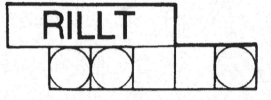

RILLT

UGGOE

UMCAUV

CELEEF

I can't tell one finny creature from the other

WHAT YOU MIGHT DO WITH THE MENU WHEN YOU'RE DINING AT A FISH RESTAURANT.

Now arrange the circled letters to form the surprise answer, as suggested by the above cartoon.

Print answer here:

JUMBLE®

Unscramble these four Jumbles, one letter to each
square, to form four ordinary words.

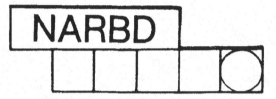

NARBD

ZEFOR

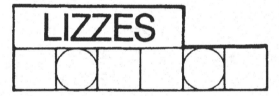

LIZZES

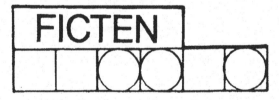

FICTEN

Who
is
he?

!

HE WENT
UNRECOGNIZED WHEN
HE HAD THIS.

Now arrange the circled letters to form the
surprise answer, as suggested by the above
cartoon.

**Print
answer
here:** HIS " ⬡⬡⬡ " ⬡⬡⬡⬡⬡⬡

JUMBLE®

Unscramble these four Jumbles, one letter to each
square, to form four ordinary words.

UGGEA

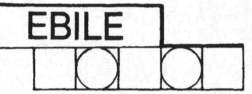

EBILE

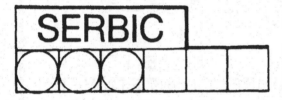

SERBIC

NITDAY

WHEN THE PRICE OF
SUGAR ESCALATED,
THE CUSTOMERS
DID THIS.

Now arrange the circled letters to form the
surprise answer, as suggested by the above
cartoon.

*Print answer
here:*

JUMBLE®

Unscramble these four Jumbles, one letter to each
square, to form four ordinary words.

MUHID

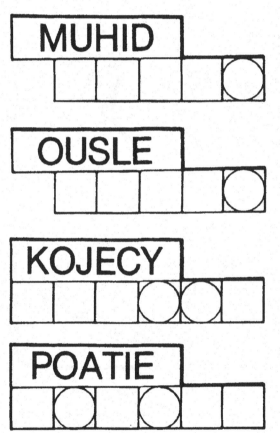

OUSLE

KOJECY

POATIE

You don't look so good

HOW HE FELT WHEN
HE FINALLY REACHED
THE VERY TOP OF
THE MOUNTAIN.

Now arrange the circled letters to form the
surprise answer, as suggested by the above
cartoon.

Print answer here:

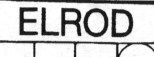

Unscramble these four Jumbles, one letter to each square, to form four ordinary words.

RUPEN

ELROD

YIVERF

TORMAR

EVERY TIME HE RAN
TWO HUNDRED YARDS,
HE ACTUALLY ONLY
DID THIS.

Now arrange the circled letters to form the surprise answer, as suggested by the above cartoon.

Print answer here: ◯◯◯◯◯ TWO ◯◯◯◯◯

JUMBLE®

Unscramble these four Jumbles, one letter to each square, to form four ordinary words.

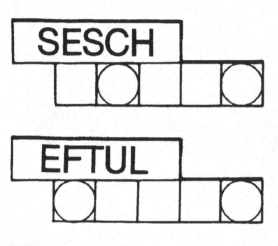

SESCH

EFTUL

KIALLA

ROYSAR

WHAT THE CHAMPION MALTED MILK MAKER THOUGHT HE GOT WHEN THE BOSS GAVE HIM A BONUS.

Now arrange the circled letters to form the surprise answer, as suggested by the above cartoon.

Print answer here: A ⬡⬡⬡⬡ "⬡⬡⬡⬡⬡"

JUMBLE®

Unscramble these four Jumbles, one letter to each
square, to form four ordinary words.

LECEX

NIDEK

CUROGH

WARTOD

AFTER GETTING TWO
COLLEGE DIPLOMAS, HE
LED A LIFE OF
CRIME UNTIL THE
COPS THREATENED
HIM WITH THIS.

Now arrange the circled letters to form the
surprise answer, as suggested by the above
cartoon.

**Print
answer
here:** A

JUMBLE®

Unscramble these four Jumbles, one letter to each square, to form four ordinary words.

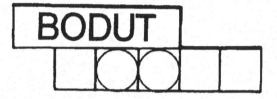

BODUT

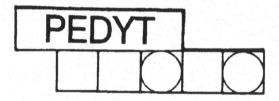

PEDYT

ENGLIS

YURTIP

Son, you're going to succeed me some day. I want you to know all about it

THE ONLY WAY TO LEARN THE COFFEE BUSINESS.

Now arrange the circled letters to form the surprise answer, as suggested by the above cartoon.

Print answer here: FROM THE "  "

JUMBLE®

Unscramble these four Jumbles, one letter to each square, to form four ordinary words.

IFFYT

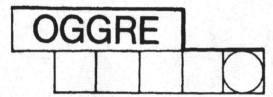

OGGRE

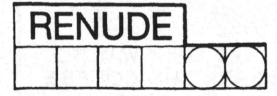

RENUDE

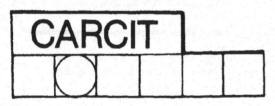

CARCIT

Now we're all set for our new home where it's warm

USED TIRES

RETREADS ARE SOLD FOR PEOPLE WHO WANT TO DO THIS.

Now arrange the circled letters to form the surprise answer, as suggested by the above cartoon.

Print answer here:

JUMBLE®

Unscramble these four Jumbles, one letter to each
square, to form four ordinary words.

VABOE

ARBIN

LEWOLF

FLUTAR

WHEN YOU BUY A
HERD OF BISON,
YOU CAN EXPECT
TO RECEIVE THIS.

Now arrange the circled letters to form the
surprise answer, as suggested by the above
cartoon.

**Print
answer
here:** A ⬭⬭⬭⬭⬭⬭⬭ " ⬭⬭⬭⬭ "

JUMBLE®

Unscramble these four Jumbles, one letter to each square, to form four ordinary words.

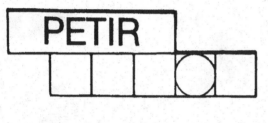

PETIR

WORNC

TRYSOF

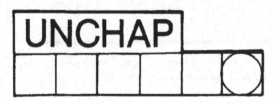

UNCHAP

WHAT THEY SERVED IN THAT RESTAURANT FAVORED BY THE KARATE CROWD.

Now arrange the circled letters to form the surprise answer, as suggested by the above cartoon.

Print answer here: "  "

JUMBLE®

Unscramble these four Jumbles, one letter to each square, to form four ordinary words.

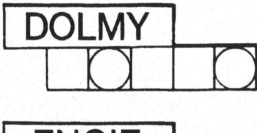

DOLMY

ENGIF

ZALBER

LEENED

You're no longer by yourself—you have us!

BANK

THAT FRIENDLY NEIGHBORHOOD BANK CATERED TO PEOPLE WHO WERE THIS.

Now arrange the circled letters to form the surprise answer, as suggested by the above cartoon.

Print answer here:  "◯◯◯◯ - ◯◯"

JUMBLE®

Unscramble these four Jumbles, one letter to each
square, to form four ordinary words.

PANCO

WENIT

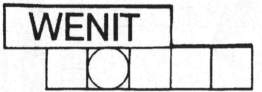

DRAWZI

QUESMO

WHY PILLOWS ARE
SO EXPENSIVE.

Now arrange the circled letters to form the
surprise answer, as suggested by the above
cartoon.

Print answer here:

JUMBLE®

Unscramble these four Jumbles, one letter to each square, to form four ordinary words.

OUMES

SATTY

REGLED

PERRIM

WHAT THEY WERE AWARDED AT THE GRADUATION CERE- MONIES AT DIVING SCHOOL.

Now arrange the circled letters to form the surprise answer, as suggested by the above cartoon.

Print answer here:

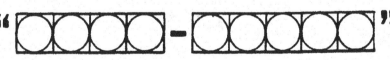

" ⬚⬚⬚⬚ - ⬚⬚⬚⬚⬚ "

JUMBLE®

Unscramble these four Jumbles, one letter to each
square, to form four ordinary words.

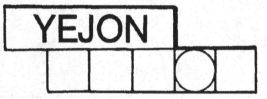

YEJON

MIRPE

CLIPSE

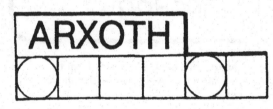

ARXOTH

IS THIS THE BEST
LUBRICANT FOR
FURNITURE WHEELS?

Now arrange the circled letters to form the
surprise answer, as suggested by the above
cartoon.

Print answer here: "⬡⬡⬡⬡⬡⬡" ⬡⬡⬡

JUMBLE®

Unscramble these four Jumbles, one letter to each square, to form four ordinary words.

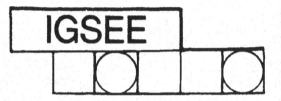

IGSEE

HESOW

HONEST AL'S

SALE

THE SMOOTHEST RUNNING THING ABOUT THAT CAR.

GOBUTH

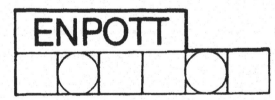

ENPOTT

Now arrange the circled letters to form the surprise answer, as suggested by the above cartoon.

Print answer here:

JUMBLE®

Unscramble these four Jumbles, one letter to each square, to form four ordinary words.

WHOYS

MAORA

PELPIN

ALFELN

Thank you, Sir Walter

ANOTHER NAME
FOR CHIVALRY.

Now arrange the circled letters to form the surprise answer, as suggested by the above cartoon.

Print answer here:

JUMBLE®

Unscramble these four Jumbles, one letter to each
square, to form four ordinary words.

TRUIF

KONET

SACCUT

DRIZAL

You'd think they'd look it up
in the encyclopedia

WHAT'S MISSING
FROM MOST HOT
DISPUTES?

Now arrange the circled letters to form the
surprise answer, as suggested by the above
cartoon.

Print answer here:

143

JUMBLE®

Unscramble these four Jumbles, one letter to each square, to form four ordinary words.

SCERS

LYGUL

TALNED

NERBAN

We're having an explosively good time

WHAT THE DYNAMITERS' ANNUAL SHINDIG WAS.

Now arrange the circled letters to form the surprise answer, as suggested by the above cartoon.

Print answer here: A ◯◯◯◯◯ ◯◯◯◯◯

JUMBLE®

Unscramble these four Jumbles, one letter to each square, to form four ordinary words.

KECHE

LOBEN

SEWBOT

NAIVED

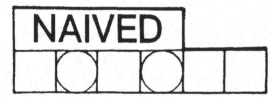

Oops!

My dear, you'll never believe what Mildred did next...

ANOTHER THING THAT PEOPLE ARE ALWAYS SPILLING.

Now arrange the circled letters to form the surprise answer, as suggested by the above cartoon.

Print answer here:

JUMBLE®

Unscramble these four Jumbles, one letter to each square, to form four ordinary words.

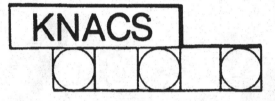

KNACS

TOYBO

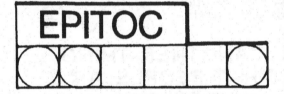

EPITOC

RANCOB

THAT HUSBAND AND WIFE KNEW EACH OTHER LIKE A BOOK---

Now arrange the circled letters to form the surprise answer, as suggested by the above cartoon.

Print answer here:

JUMBLE®

Unscramble these four Jumbles, one letter to each square, to form four ordinary words.

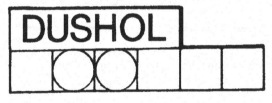

KLUFE

ATAGE

RAHWTT

DUSHOL

Did I disturb you, Mary Ann?

Oh, no! I am just taking a bath and trying to wash my hair

SOMETHING ONE'S IN WHEN ONE'S NOT IN ANYTHING ELSE.

Now arrange the circled letters to form the surprise answer, as suggested by the above cartoon.

Print answer here: THE ⬭⬭⬭⬭⬭⬭⬭⬭⬭⬭

JUMBLE®

Unscramble these four Jumbles, one letter to each
square, to form four ordinary words.

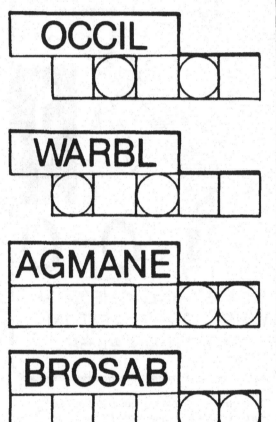

OCCIL

WARBL

AGMANE

BROSAB

WHAT BUILDING
THAT BIG TUNNEL
MUST HAVE BEEN.

Now arrange the circled letters to form the
surprise answer, as suggested by the above
cartoon.

Print answer here:

148

JUMBLE®

Unscramble these four Jumbles, one letter to each square, to form four ordinary words.

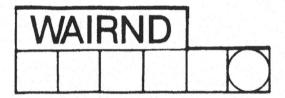

THE SELFISH FARM-HAND HAD TROUBLE MILKING THE COW, BECAUSE HE HAD NO REGARD FOR THE FEELING OF THIS.

Now arrange the circled letters to form the surprise answer, as suggested by the above cartoon.

Print answer here:

JUMBLE®

Unscramble these four Jumbles, one letter to each square, to form four ordinary words.

URSOE

TIPAL

PHONIS

SAWLAY

HOW TO MAIL
AN UMBRELLA.

Now arrange the circled letters to form the surprise answer, as suggested by the above cartoon.

***Print
answer
here:*** BY "⬡⬡⬡⬡⬡⬡⬡" ⬡⬡⬡⬡

Unscramble these four Jumbles, one letter to each square, to form four ordinary words.

BYRIN

GUZAE

LEPPUR

ENDECT

THE DIARY IS
THE BOOK WHERE
ALL HER SECRETS
ARE THIS.

Now arrange the circled letters to form the surprise answer, as suggested by the above cartoon.

Print answer here: "  "

JUMBLE®

Unscramble these four Jumbles, one letter to each square, to form four ordinary words.

GLEEY

YOHBB

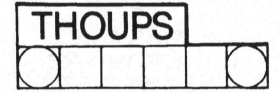

THOUPS

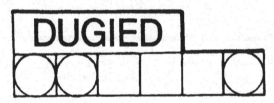

DUGIED

WHAT THE ANT DID WHEN HE SAW THE ANTEATER.

Now arrange the circled letters to form the surprise answer, as suggested by the above cartoon.

Print answer here:

JUMBLE®

Unscramble these four Jumbles, one letter to each
square, to form four ordinary words.

DELAL

ORXYP

UNBRAU

CYTHAC

SOME SAILORS WHO
MAKE THEIR LIVING
ON WATER SELDOM
DO THIS.

Now arrange the circled letters to form the
surprise answer, as suggested by the above
cartoon.

**Print
answer
here:** ⬡⬡⬡⬡ IT ON ⬡⬡⬡⬡

JUMBLE®

Unscramble these four Jumbles, one letter to each square, to form four ordinary words.

INNOO

TEBER

CLOUNK

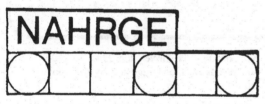

NAHRGE

HER CHOICE OF HUSBAND SHOWED BETTER TASTE THAN THIS.

Now arrange the circled letters to form the surprise answer, as suggested by the above cartoon.

Print answer here:

JUMBLE®

Unscramble these four Jumbles, one letter to each square, to form four ordinary words.

KEEVO

RAWLD

PANOWE

ERRTAY

We're going to the opera tonight

NO! NO! NO!

HER STRONG WILL DOMINATED THIS.

Now arrange the circled letters to form the surprise answer, as suggested by the above cartoon.

Print answer here: HIS  " ' "

JUMBLE.

Unscramble these four Jumbles, one letter to each
square, to form four ordinary words.

NAISE

SIDAY

BEFILE

MOUFAS

Guess
SHE'S going
to do the
proposing

WOMEN USE
PERFUME BECAUSE
SOME MEN ARE
EASILY THIS.

Now arrange the circled letters to form the
surprise answer, as suggested by the above
cartoon.

Print answer here:

BY
THE

Unscramble these four Jumbles, one letter to each
square, to form four ordinary words.

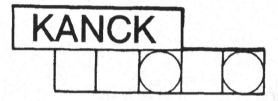

KANCK

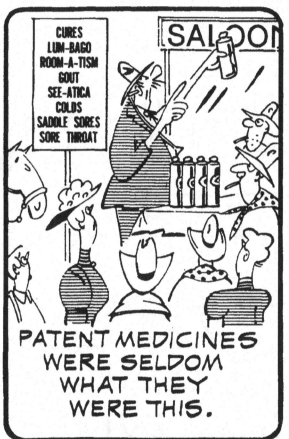

CURES
LUM-BAGO
ROOM-A-TISM
GOUT
SEE-ATICA
COLDS
SADDLE SORES
SORE THROAT

SALOON

ECHLE

PATENT MEDICINES
WERE SELDOM
WHAT THEY
WERE THIS.

NUCHEQ

DEGUBB

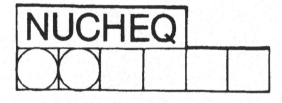

Now arrange the circled letters to form the
surprise answer, as suggested by the above
cartoon.

**Print
answer
here:**

" " UP
TO

JUMBLE®

Unscramble these four Jumbles, one letter to each square, to form four ordinary words.

PHACT

INYPP

ROZNEF

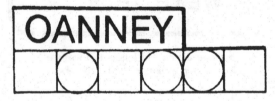

OANNEY

They've never been right yet

THE WEATHER BUREAU MIGHT SOMETIMES BE DESCRIBED AS THIS KIND OF AN AGENCY.

Now arrange the circled letters to form the surprise answer, as suggested by the above cartoon.

Print answer here: "⬡⬡⬡ – ⬡⬡⬡⬡⬡⬡⬡"

JUMBLE®

Unscramble these four Jumbles, one letter to each square, to form four ordinary words.

FODOL

TELIT

DUBUSE

GENJAL

I could...

But then again, I could also save my money

RACING

HOW TO ASSURE THAT YOU DON'T LOSE MONEY AT THE TRACK.

Now arrange the circled letters to form the surprise answer, as suggested by the above cartoon.

Print answer here:

JUMBLE®

Unscramble these four Jumbles, one letter to each
square, to form four ordinary words.

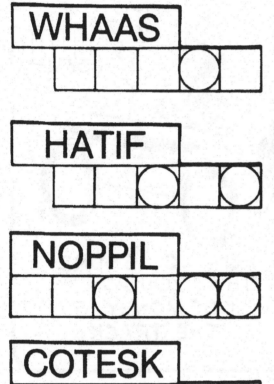

WHAAS

HATIF

NOPPIL

COTESK

RICH RELATIVES
LEFT HIM A YACHT,
AND EVER SINCE
HE'S BEEN TALKING
ABOUT THIS.

Now arrange the circled letters to form the
surprise answer, as suggested by the above
cartoon.

Print answer here: HIS " ◯◯◯ ◯◯◯◯◯ "

JUMBLE®

Unscramble these four Jumbles, one letter to each
square, to form four ordinary words.

UNFYN

PUMBY

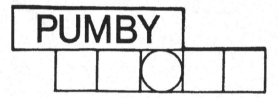

KUEBER

OTHPRY

WHAT HAPPENED
WHEN NYLON
STOCKINGS WERE
FIRST INTRODUCED?

Now arrange the circled letters to form the
surprise answer, as suggested by the above
cartoon.

**Print
answer
here:**   THERE " ◯◯◯ " ◯◯ ◯◯◯◯◯
WAS A

JUMBLE®

Unscramble these four Jumbles, one letter to each
square, to form four ordinary words.

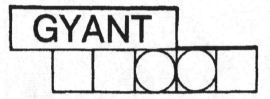

GYANT

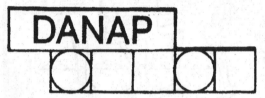

DANAP

GURFEE

PURROA

A GOOD HAM-
BURGER IS MADE
FROM THIS.

Now arrange the circled letters to form the
surprise answer, as suggested by the above
cartoon.

Print answer here: THE

JUMBLE®

JAMBOREE

Challenger
Puzzles

JUMBLE®

Unscramble these six Jumbles, one letter to each square, to form six ordinary words.

THAAMS

BUCHYB

SLIRGY

UNEEVA

SIPVLE

LENPOY

He's very successful

THE ENCYCLOPEDIA
SALESMAN WAS
INVOLVED IN THIS.

Now arrange the circled letters to form the surprise answer, as suggested by the above cartoon.

PRINT YOUR ANSWER IN THE CIRCLES BELOW

A

JUMBLE®

Unscramble these six Jumbles, one letter to each square, to form six ordinary words.

THROOC

ENFADE

HINSIF

LUMUTT

TURUNE

NUPREY

Hey, that's for our customers!

WHY THE COOK WHO NIBBLED ALL DAY GOT FIRED.

Now arrange the circled letters to form the surprise answer, as suggested by the above cartoon.

PRINT YOUR ANSWER IN THE CIRCLES BELOW

HE ⃝⃝⃝ ⃝⃝⃝⃝ THE ⃝⃝⃝⃝⃝⃝⃝

JUMBLE®

Unscramble these six Jumbles, one letter to each square, to form six ordinary words.

VOGNER

GUTTAH

YETHIG

UMLOVE

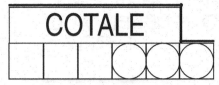
COTALE

THEZIN

Good pictures come from good development

MAKES SENSE ONLY FOR A PHOTOGRAPHER.

3/29

Now arrange the circled letters to form the surprise answer, as suggested by the above cartoon.

PRINT YOUR ANSWER IN THE CIRCLES BELOW

A

166

JUMBLE®

Unscramble these six Jumbles, one letter to each square, to form six ordinary words.

LEEXAH

CUTOLC

FLUEYE

RITAUN

PANKID

CORRET

4-5

Take the bum out!

Barkeep, we need another one

WHAT THE BASEBALL FANS CALLED FOR WHEN THE BEER RAN OUT.

Now arrange the circled letters to form the surprise answer, as suggested by the above cartoon.

PRINT YOUR ANSWER IN THE CIRCLES BELOW

A ⬡⬡⬡⬡⬡⬡ "⬡⬡⬡⬡⬡⬡⬡"

167

JUMBLE®

Unscramble these six Jumbles, one letter to each square, to form six ordinary words.

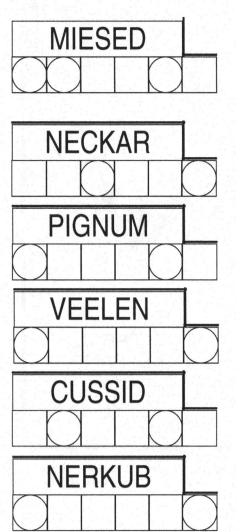

MIESED

NECKAR

PIGNUM

VEELEN

CUSSID

NERKUB

I'm dying to live someplace where we can stay warm

6-7

A COLD NIGHT CAN LEAD TO THIS.

Now arrange the circled letters to form the surprise answer, as suggested by the above cartoon.

PRINT YOUR ANSWER IN THE CIRCLES BELOW

A "⬚⬚⬚⬚⬚⬚⬚⬚⬚" ⬚⬚⬚⬚⬚⬚⬚

Unscramble these six Jumbles, one letter to each square, to form six ordinary words.

IMLISE

SEXOPE

BROSAB

NITTEY

LENCAG

QUALEP

It's just like their natural habitat

WHAT THE ZOO PROVIDED THE GRIZZLIES.

Now arrange the circled letters to form the surprise answer, as suggested by the above cartoon.

PRINT YOUR ANSWER IN THE CIRCLES BELOW

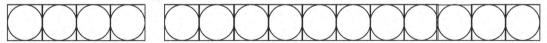

JUMBLE.

Unscramble these six Jumbles, one letter to each
square, to form six ordinary words.

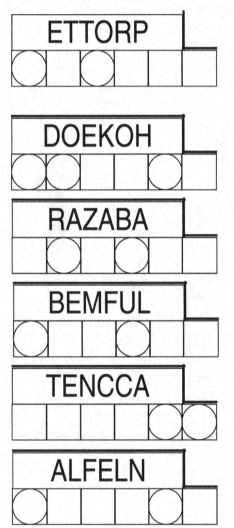

ETTORP

DOEKOH

RAZABA

BEMFUL

TENCCA

ALFELN

—— Four meters
to go

FINISH
LINE

6
21

A LOSING RUN-
NER WANTS TO
GET HERE.

Now arrange the circled letters to form the
surprise answer, as suggested by the above
cartoon.

PRINT YOUR ANSWER IN THE CIRCLES BELOW

THE " "

JUMBLE®

Unscramble these six Jumbles, one letter to each square, to form six ordinary words.

YADDLE

CARCIT

GOLLAB

SMIDOW

REDDEG

EISORE

It's from Tom and Betty

6-28

WHAT THEY SENT BACK FROM THE TROP-ICAL ISLAND.

Now arrange the circled letters to form the surprise answer, as suggested by the above cartoon.

PRINT YOUR ANSWER IN THE CIRCLES BELOW

" ⬡⬡⬡⬡⬡⬡⬡⬡ " ⬡⬡⬡⬡⬡⬡⬡⬡

JUMBLE®

Unscramble these six Jumbles, one letter to each square, to form six ordinary words.

DRATOW

UCCSAU

SLAPOT

RAAPPE

TIFLLE

DEELMY

5-10

EASY TO ENJOY
IN A HOTEL'S
POSH QUARTERS.

Now arrange the circled letters to form the surprise answer, as suggested by the above cartoon.

PRINT YOUR ANSWER IN THE CIRCLES BELOW

JUMBLE®

Unscramble these six Jumbles, one letter to each square, to form six ordinary words.

KIRBEC

SACCUT

GROAND

PLALAP

CHABRE

COALJE

WELCOME TO THE UNIVERSITY

You're taking four courses

5/17

USING A CHARGE CARD FOR TUITION GOT HER THIS.

Now arrange the circled letters to form the surprise answer, as suggested by the above cartoon.

PRINT YOUR ANSWER IN THE CIRCLES BELOW

173

JUMBLE®

Unscramble these six Jumbles, one letter to each square, to form six ordinary words.

FANNIT

CADAFE

GROCED

REENOC

DEKBEC

FOTEEF

They really work hard

5/24

ALWAYS GIVEN BY AN ORCHESTRA.

Now arrange the circled letters to form the surprise answer, as suggested by the above cartoon.

PRINT YOUR ANSWER IN THE CIRCLES BELOW

A " ◯◯◯◯◯◯◯ - ◯◯ " ◯◯◯◯◯◯◯

174

JUMBLE®

Unscramble these six Jumbles, one letter to each square, to form six ordinary words.

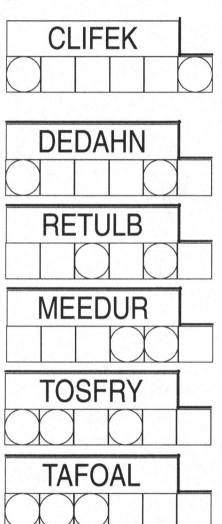

CLIFEK

DEDAHN

RETULB

MEEDUR

TOSFRY

TAFOAL

!!#%**! Awwk!

What did he call me?

A FOUL-MOUTHED PARROT CAN DO THIS TO A GUEST.

5/31

Now arrange the circled letters to form the surprise answer, as suggested by the above cartoon.

PRINT YOUR ANSWER IN THE CIRCLES BELOW

HIS

JUMBLE®

Unscramble these six Jumbles, one letter to each square, to form six ordinary words.

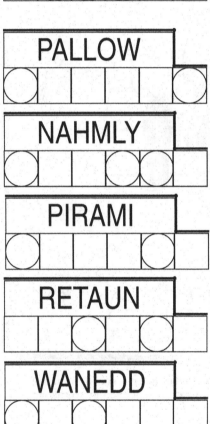

YADLAM

PALLOW

NAHMLY

PIRAMI

RETAUN

WANEDD

It hurts to do this, but the bills are due

TELLER

4/12

THE RESULT OF TAPPING YOUR SAVINGS ACCOUNT.

Now arrange the circled letters to form the surprise answer, as suggested by the above cartoon.

PRINT YOUR ANSWER IN THE CIRCLES BELOW

JUMBLE®

Unscramble these six Jumbles, one letter to each
square, to form six ordinary words.

RITHEM

REEMIP

REFUGI

WHACES

DILERB

RITTHY

For the best
in the school...

WHAT THE AN-
NUAL PENMAN-
SHIP AWARD
CEREMONY WAS
CALLED.

Now arrange the circled letters to form the
surprise answer, as suggested by the above
cartoon.

PRINT YOUR ANSWER IN THE CIRCLES BELOW

A

177

JUMBLE®

Unscramble these six Jumbles, one letter to each square, to form six ordinary words.

DAJEGG

REFLAT

TANTIA

YORCAN

TYLPEN

MAGITS

She's gorgeous

4/26

WHERE THE MODEL ENDED UP AFTER SIGNING A BIG CON- TRACT.

Now arrange the circled letters to form the surprise answer, as suggested by the above cartoon.

JUMBLE®

Unscramble these six Jumbles, one letter to each square, to form six ordinary words.

POWNEA

YESGER

DREEME

PICHER

DELOON

TRIVUE

This way, boys

He knows
his stuff

5/3

THE HERD FOL-
LOWED THE
TRAIL BOSS BE-
CAUSE HE WAS----

Now arrange the circled letters to form the surprise answer, as suggested by the above cartoon.

PRINT YOUR ANSWER IN THE CIRCLES BELOW

A "⬡⬡⬡⬡⬡⬡-⬡⬡⬡⬡" ⬡⬡⬡⬡⬡⬡

JUMBLE®

Unscramble these six Jumbles, one letter to each
square, to form six ordinary words.

DACROW

WALCOL

GROOFT

FOLFAY

ATWIRE

KALLIA

Okay--you asked for it!

2-15

ERUPTS WHEN
APES GET ANGRY.

Now arrange the circled letters to form the
surprise answer, as suggested by the above
cartoon.

PRINT YOUR ANSWER IN THE CIRCLES BELOW

JUMBLE®

Unscramble these six Jumbles, one letter to each square, to form six ordinary words.

MEEZYN

FRIMAF

GATNIC

NACINE

PERMUB

YANJUT

They sound
great

2/22

WHAT THE
MOVERS WERE
GOOD AT.

Now arrange the circled letters to form the surprise answer, as suggested by the above cartoon.

PRINT YOUR ANSWER IN THE CIRCLES BELOW

A

JUMBLE.

Unscramble these six Jumbles, one letter to each square, to form six ordinary words.

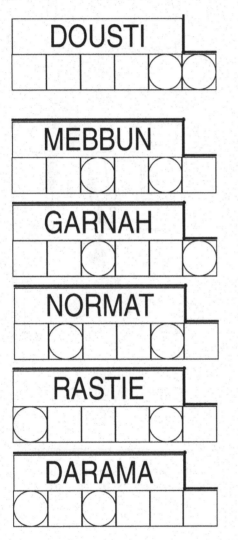

DOUSTI

MEBBUN

GARNAH

NORMAT

RASTIE

DARAMA

THEY WERE SEEN
IN ITALY'S
BIGGEST CITY.

Now arrange the circled letters to form the surprise answer, as suggested by the above cartoon.

PRINT YOUR ANSWER IN THE CIRCLES BELOW

JUMBLE®

Unscramble these six Jumbles, one letter to each square, to form six ordinary words.

NEETIC

SNUFIL

BREMME

BEJOCT

SPENOR

ZEBRAL

LAWYERS AND
JUDGES MIGHT
HAVE THESE.

Now arrange the circled letters to form the surprise answer, as suggested by the above cartoon.

PRINT YOUR ANSWER IN THE CIRCLES BELOW

"◯◯◯◯◯◯" ◯◯◯◯◯◯◯◯◯◯◯◯◯

183

ANSWERS

1. **Jumbles:** WHOSE PAGAN RUBBER BESTOW
   Answer: Such fruit is not considered much good when unobtainable—SOUR GRAPES

2. **Jumbles:** PLUSH DOWNY INDICT FOSSIL
   Answer: Could be all that fighter ever licked—HIS WOUNDS

3. **Jumbles:** HOBBY SOUSE AMBUSH INFANT
   Answer: He has succeeded in business by being a man of great cultivation—OF HIS BOSS

4. **Jumbles:** FIFTY BOOTY LIMPID BEFORE
   Answer: Such a warning sounds "pointless"—A TIP-OFF

5. **Jumbles:** PIANO LUSTY MOSAIC CLERGY
   Answer: Sounds like a dramatic last word—"CURTAIN"

6. **Jumbles:** LEAKY BLAZE CHUBBY POLICE
   Answer: Using this, a golfer should keep the first part on the second—"EYE-BALL"

7. **Jumbles:** LOUSY TEASE MALICE HEIFER
   Answer: What the potter's art consists of—"FEATS" OF CLAY

8. **Jumbles:** MIRTH CRANK THRESH UNFAIR
   Answer: What his "position" in France gives him the right to vote—"FRANC-HIS-E"

9. **Jumbles:** SNACK PIPER MASCOT NICELY
   Answer: They hush up reports of murders—SILENCERS

10. **Jumbles:** HAZEL CRAWL OFFSET MOHAIR
    Answer: When you give the answers in "round" numbers, you're apt to come up with this—ALL ZEROS

11. **Jumbles:** EXCEL PANIC NEPHEW ANKLET
    Answer: Could it be a place to live if you've got time?—A CELL

12. **Jumbles:** YACHT OPERA INWARD ASSAIL
    Answer: This musical composition "involves" harps at first—"RHAPS-ODY"

13. **Jumbles:** CARGO FOCUS UPSHOT TROPHY
    Answer: What the rookie G.I. was told to take in order to get to the barber's in the quickest possible way—A SHORT CUT

14. **Jumbles:** BORAX FORTY PELVIS OPAQUE
    Answer: Could be a sport "connected" with the clergy—"PASTOR"

15. **Jumbles:** MAUVE LIMIT LEEWAY WEASEL
    Answer: Everything is "soaked" in the billfold—"W-ALL-ET"

16. **Jumbles:** BARON LOFTY SUBMIT GRISLY
    Answer: What "Jack and the Beanstalk" is—A TALL STORY

17. **Jumbles:** TASTY ARDOR YEARLY BOUGHT
    Answer: What they paid the king who wrote a book—A ROYALTY

18. **Jumbles:** PILOT GLOAT SWIVEL CHERUB
    Answer: An insult that sometimes seems rather slight—A "SLIGHT"

19. **Jumbles:** PRUNE GUILD NEARBY MANIAC
    Answer: What you might get when you overly indulge—A BULGE

20. **Jumbles:** HEAVY FOYER LAGOON QUAINT
    Answer: This sure made her face red!—ROUGE

21. **Jumbles:** FORCE QUEEN EXODUS PIGEON
    Answer: "I am the first one in the grammar class"—"PERSON"

22. **Jumbles:** CAPON TAWNY POLICY GRUBBY
    Answer: Many people buy on time, but few do this—PAY THAT WAY

23. **Jumbles:** ERUPT ROUSE CAUCUS JAILED
    Answer: Take down for a customer—REDUCE THE PRICE

24. **Jumbles:** SLANT GOOSE TYPIST SKEWER
    Answer: What the anxiety-ridden soprano was evidently suffering from—"SONG-STRESS"

25. **Jumbles:** YEARN ONION STUDIO THEORY
    Answer: What happened to the farmer's cattle?—NO ONE'S HERD

26. **Jumbles:** RHYME VYING SALUTE NEWEST
    Answer: The Constitution guarantees free speech, but it doesn't guarantee this—LISTENERS

27. **Jumbles:** OCTET VIRUS MUSEUM BALLET
    Answer: She married a banker because his virtues exceeded this—HIS "VAULTS" (faults)

28. **Jumbles:** CLUCK ADAPT EYELID DAMPEN
    Answer: Some compliments are not so much candid as this—"CANDIED"

29. **Jumbles:** BERYL KEYED ANKLET CUDGEL
    Answer: The first thing a man often runs into with a new car—DEBT

30. **Jumbles:** COUPE GRIPE THROAT POLICE
    Answer: What a successful pickpocket always tries to get next to—THE "RIGHT" PEOPLE

31. **Jumbles:** BELLE TROTH LUNACY OUTWIT
    Answer: All-night conversations tend to be dullest just before this—THE "YAWN" (the dawn)

32. **Jumbles:** SOOTY GULCH ASSURE JOVIAL
    Answer: What a Boy Scout becomes at a certain age—A GIRL "SCOUT"

33. **Jumbles:** GAILY IDIOM JUNGLE VIRILE
    Answer: He wouldn't be in such a hurry if he knew he was this—DRIVING TO JAIL

34. **Jumbles:** CHANT LANKY POLICY BUCKLE
    Answer: What the chiropractor's fees amounted to—"BACK" PAY

35. **Jumbles:** INLET MOSSY GOVERN FACING
    Answer: What goes on and on and has "oneself" in the middle?—AN "ON-I-ON"

36. **Jumbles:** POACH FINNY HAGGLE WEASEL
    Answer: What the ballplayer turned farmer found himself doing—CHASING A "FOWL" (foul)

37. **Jumbles:** ROACH STOIC LETHAL WEAKEN
    Answer: What the man in charge of the doughnut factory said he was—THE "HOLE" WORKS

38. **Jumbles:** BOUND DUCAT CYMBAL PREFER
    Answer: Another thing you can't take with you—YOUR LAP

39. **Jumbles:** PARCH EXTOL AWHILE MINGLE
    Answer: What tune did the teakettle whistle?-"HOME ON THE RANGE"

40. **Jumbles:** DRONE CREEK KERNEL ADRIFT
    Answer: The fear that relatives are coming to stay—"KIN DREAD" (kindred)

41. **Jumbles:** PRIOR GLOAT PURVEY TURBAN
    Answer: He was so lazy he didn't give a rap, even when this did—OPPORTUNITY

42. **Jumbles:** CYCLE GAUDY FAMILY DELUXE
    Answer: What the marriage counselor was always in the middle of—A MUDDLE

43. **Jumbles:** SOUSE GASSY POLISH DETAIN
    Answer: For the fanatic collector, this was an obsession—POSSESSION

44. **Jumbles:** KNEEL AXIOM HERALD SATIRE
    Answer: His footprints on the sands of time left only this—THE MARKS OF A HEEL

45. **Jumbles:** BATCH PILOT STYLUS HEIFER
    Answer: Some people don't trust the ocean, because they're convinced there's something—"FISHY" ABOUT IT

46. **Jumbles:** RAVEN PIECE REVERE SIMILE
    Answer: Some members of the rising generation could rise even higher if they would do this—RISE EARLIER

47. **Jumbles:** FAIRY LOVER PARADE TIDBIT
    Answer: A deadbeat sticks to his friends until this—"DEBT" DO THEM PART

48. **Jumbles:** EXULT MUSTY SLEEPY BEHAVE
Answer: What a car brings out in some men—
THE BEAST

49. **Jumbles:** NAÏVE KNIFE LOCALE SQUIRM
Answer: He believed in marrying a woman for her figure, especially when it did this—RAN INTO MILLIONS

50. **Jumbles:** LINEN BUXOM FRACAS MALICE
Answer: What they experienced when the life of the party finally went home—"COMIC RELIEF"

51. **Jumbles:** FETCH QUEUE AMAZON CANNED
Answer: Fit to be eaten except in this—EDEN

52. **Jumbles:** FAVOR CLOVE NOTIFY MOTION
Answer: What the bigamist took—ONE TOO MANY

53. **Jumbles:** FLUID HEDGE TURKEY POLITE
Answer: What position does a monster play on the hockey team?—"GHOUL-IE"

54. **Jumbles:** LATHE CHALK HAZARD WALNUT
Answer: Needs to know your zodiacal sign before she tells you this—WHAT YOU WANT TO HEAR

55. **Jumbles:** ACUTE MAIZE ZINNIA STURDY
Answer: The favorite fish at that old Russian court—"CZAR-DINES"

56. **Jumbles:** MINCE ALTAR DEPUTY MAROON
Answer: When the new favorite arrived at the zoo, there was this among the kids—"PANDA-MONIUM"

57. **Jumbles:** LOWLY SWISH GAIETY CAUGHT
Answer: "A piece of beef, and make it lean"—
"WHICH WAY?"

58. **Jumbles:** SLANT HUMAN EQUITY PLAGUE
Answer: Another name for sarcasm—"QUIP LASH"

59. **Jumbles:** NOOSE PIPER KIMONO HERMIT
Answer: What she thought she'd do when her boyfriend's car needed a new muffler—KNIT HIM ONE

60. **Jumbles:** GIVEN HIKER PURIFY MAYHEM
Answer: What the man who invented rope built for himself—A HUGE "HEMP-IRE"

61. **Jumbles:** PUDGY CRIME RABBIT DEFINE
Answer: Hair on a man's head might be parted when it's not this—DEPARTED

62. **Jumbles:** ALIVE EMBER KINDLY INJURE
Answer: How the coal digger's favorite music was played—IN A "MINER" KEY

63. **Jumbles:** ENEMY COUGH VIABLE DEVICE
Answer: Why Dracula died of a broken heart—
HE HAD LOVED IN "VEIN"

64. **Jumbles:** UNCLE BAKED HELMET DRIVEL
Answer: What Don Juan was—A BIG "DAME HUNTER"

65. **Jumbles:** TITLE LAUGH FURROW HELIUM
Answer: Why he at so much bread—
HE WAS IN "LOAF" WITH IT (in love with it)

66. **Jumbles:** DOUGH FLOOD LEAVEN UTMOST
Answer: A conversation between a traffic cop and a driver—A MONOLOGUE

67. **Jumbles:** MERGE SHAKY DECADE LAWFUL
Answer: When you pat a man on the back he often end up with this—A SWELLED HEAD

68. **Jumbles:** LEAVE HELLO SUBTLY TRUSTY
Answer: What they said it was when that Russian dancer turned out to be a spy—A BALLET "RUSE"

69. **Jumbles:** ENACT PAYEE VERBAL LAVISH
Answer: A welcome guest knows when to do this—
"LEAVE & LET LIVE"

70. **Jumbles:** SNARL LLAMA COUGAR ORIGIN
Answer: That egotistical cynic saw nothing good in the world, without the aid of this—A MIRROR

71. **Jumbles:** IDIOT FUZZY BROKER ATTAIN
Answer: What an astronaut has to be before he really starts working on the job—"FIRED"

72. **Jumbles:** POKER TEASE HYMNAL SURETY
Answer: What the game of polo involves a lot of—
"HORSE PLAY"

73. **Jumbles:** TONIC ALBUM KNOTTY SLEIGH
Answer: Why they call them "tellers" at banks—MONEY ALWAYS "TALKS"

74. **Jumbles:** FELON LUCID WALRUS CLOTHE
Answer: What the young couple got when they went to the marriage counselor—A "WED-UCATION"

75. **Jumbles:** HOIST PARTY BUTTON DETACH
Answer: He aimed to please, but he was this—
A BAD SHOT

76. **Jumbles:** SILKY HONOR CRAYON HUMBLE
Answer: If you want to succeed as a violinist, this is how you have to get involved with your music—
UP TO YOUR CHIN

77. **Jumbles:** CIVIL BATHE TROUGH RELISH
Answer: Another name for writer's cramp—
"AUTHORITIS" (arthritis)

78. **Jumbles:** ELITE ANNUL FLUNKY COMPEL
Answer: How he got the job—BY "KIN-FLUENCE"

79. **Jumbles:** BOWER PROBE TEAPOT FIDDLE
Answer: The hypochondriac changed doctors when he started to do this—FEEL BETTER

80. **Jumbles:** RODEO LIVEN WORTHY EMBALM
Answer: He offered to help with the lawn because he needed this—"MOWER MONEY" (more money)

81. **Jumbles:** BIRCH SWASH PONDER MARVEL
Answer: A woman without a heart might make a fool of a man without this—A HEAD

82. **Jumbles:** PIETY ICILY TROLLY BAFFLE
Answer: His inability to tell the truth turned out to be this for him—A "LIE-ABILITY"

83. **Jumbles:** SWAMP CHICK PLURAL BURLAP
Answer: The door to success is usually open to people who have lots of this—PUSH & PULL

84. **Jumbles:** APRON FORCE CANOPY HECKLE
Answer: What the arrogant insect was—
A COCKY ROACH

85. **Jumbles:** OPIUM FISHY SLOUCH NINETY
Answer: When he proposed that they get married, she told him that the outcome would depend on this—
HIS INCOME

86. **Jumbles:** TAFFY HONEY EIGHTY CONCUR
Answer: You show poise when you raise your eyebrows instead of this—THE ROOF

87. **Jumbles:** GLEAM FORTY SULTRY PULPIT
Answer: If your "pancake" makeup isn't all you expected it to be, you might try adding this—MAPLE SYRUP

88. **Jumbles:** MINER NAVAL STRONG ORIOLE
Answer: The right time to buy a boat—
WHEN THERE'S A "SAIL" ON IT

89. **Jumbles:** WAGON CLOAK FLATLY RADIUS
Answer: That so-called financial advisor is always ready to back his judgment with this—YOUR LAST DOLLAR

90. **Jumbles:** FENCE DRAFT HOPPER THRESH
Answer: If someone is now celebrating his birthday, there's no gift like this—THE "PRESENT"

91. **Jumbles:** PIVOT DOWNY FAULTY BECOME
Answer: Where you might see a shooting star—
IN A COWBOY FILM

92. **Jumbles:** CRAFT ELDER BAZAAR FINERY
Answer: What he said when he couldn't find a decent pair of socks in his drawer—"DARN" IT!

93. **Jumbles:** JOINT FLOOR LOCKET VANDAL
Answer: What the coach kept saying to the team of zombies—LOOK ALIVE!

94. **Jumbles:** FUROR TABOO COWARD BASKET
Answer: Another name for newly hatched termites—
"BABES IN THE WOOD"

95. **Jumbles:** ELUDE HAVEN STUPID NATURE
Answer: The "tense" he used most frequently when making speeches—"PRE-TENSE"

96. **Jumbles:** PEACE DAILY CURFEW SMOKER
Answer: Could that smart cookie be this?—A WISE "CRACKER"

97. **Jumbles:** INEPT GUILT PIRATE FORBID
Answer: What people sometimes were during the Stone Age—"PETRIFIED"

98. **Jumbles:** SKULK LURID FAIRLY GENDER
Answer: What she called him when he went back on his promise to buy her a mink—A FINK

99. **Jumbles:** THYME IMPEL POCKET RADISH
Answer: Many a man is burned by picking up this—A HOT TIP

100. **Jumbles:** CHIDE AWOKE DONKEY WAITER
Answer: That conceited guy thinks that if he had never been born, the world would do this—WONDER WHY

101. **Jumbles:** VAPOR JUMPY PAUPER YEARLY
Answer: The beginning of a dog's life might start when someone experiences this—PUPPY LOVE

102. **Jumbles:** RANCH FAULT HEARSE LIMPID
Answer: What that precociously bright baby was—A FLASH IN THE "PRAM"

103. **Jumbles:** IDIOT BOUND PSYCHE FATHOM
Answer: What that graduation picture was—A PHOTO FINISH

104. **Jumbles:** WHEAT DIRTY SYSTEM FOSSIL
Answer: Should a car with automatic drive be entrusted to someone who's this?—"SHIFTLESS"

105. **Jumbles:** AGLOW WOVEN NOODLE MOTIVE
Answer: When they gave that huge banquet in China, how much did the food weigh?—"WONTON" (one ton)

106. **Jumbles:** SHEAF CLOUT FUMBLE TREATY
Answer: Horseback riding is a sport that sometimes makes the novice feel this—BETTER OFF

107. **Jumbles:** DECAY LIGHT CALMLY BAKERY
Answer: What there was plenty of after the post office caught fire—"BLACK MAIL"

108. **Jumbles:** QUEER FAINT BENIGN TANKER
Answer: He thinks he's going places when he's really this—BEING "TAKEN"

109. **Jumbles:** GUARD HITCH STICKY COSTLY
Answer: What to say to the man who thinks he can afford a boat like that—"YACHTS" OF LUCK

110. **Jumbles:** ACRID FUSSY REALTY TEMPER
Answer: He wanted to be an astronaut, but they said all he had taken up in school was this—"SPACE"

111. **Jumbles:** PIANO TULIP GUILTY PUNDIT
Answer: A diet is something you keep putting off while you keep this—PUTTING ON

112. **Jumbles:** OPERA MOUNT SPONGE HELPER
Answer: What that tall beachcomber was—A LONG "SHOREMAN"

113. **Jumbles:** ICING GUILE SINFUL FORMAL
Answer: People who go all out often end up this way—ALL IN

114. **Jumbles:** CRUSH UPPER SPRUCE POORLY
Answer: An elopement sometimes results when man proposes and future mother-in-law does this—OPPOSES

115. **Jumbles:** ORBIT APPLY CHARGE BIGAMY
Answer: Candles on birthday cakes help people make this—"LIGHT" OF THEIR AGE

116. **Jumbles:** QUEEN DUSKY BRUTAL SMUDGE
Answer: How automobiles moved before anyone thought of using lubricating oil—THEY JUST SQUEAKED BY

117. **Jumbles:** FLANK VALVE RATHER SUBWAY
Answer: What's the environment like when you sleep alongside your horse?—VERY STABLE

118. **Jumbles:** PECAN GOURD UNTRUE NEPHEW
Answer: What happened to the restaurant that served those substandard submarine sandwiches?—IT WENT UNDER

119. **Jumbles:** GRIME SPURN KENNEL INSIST
Answer: What the cops looked for when there was a robbery at the sausage factory—THE MISSING "LINK"

120. **Jumbles:** GLADE APART COOKIE ENOUGH
Answer: What those stray dogs enjoyed most at dinnertime—"POUND" CAKE

121. **Jumbles:** CABLE GROUP BALSAM FUNGUS
Answer: What that heroic fireman became—"FLAMOUS"

122. **Jumbles:** EXILE LAPEL PRISON COMPLY
Answer: What you might find at that mom and pop tire shop—A NICE "SPARE"

123. **Jumbles:** ANNOY PLAID WALLOP TWINGE
Answer: What you might end up with from too much housecleaning—A WINDOW "PAIN"

124. **Jumbles:** TRILL GOUGE VACUUM FLEECE
Answer: What you might do with the menu when you're dining at a fish restaurant—"MULLET" OVER

125. **Jumbles:** BRAND FROZE SIZZLE INFECT
Answer: He went unrecognized when he had this—HIS "FEZ" LIFTED

126. **Jumbles:** GAUGE BELIE SCRIBE DAINTY
Answer: When the price of sugar escalated, the customers did this—RAISED "CANE"

127. **Jumbles:** HUMID LOUSE JOCKEY OPIATE
Answer: How he felt when he finally reached the very top of the mountain-"PEAK-ED"

128. **Jumbles:** PRUNE OLDER VERIFY MORTAR
Answer: Every time he ran two hundred yards, he actually only did this—MOVED TWO FEET

129. **Jumbles:** CHESS FLUTE ALKALI ROSARY
Answer: What the champion malted milk maker thought he got when the boss gave him a bonus—A FAIR "SHAKE"

130. **Jumbles:** EXCEL INKED GROUCH TOWARD
Answer: After getting two college diplomas, he led a life of crime until the cops threatened him with this–A THIRD DEGREE

131. **Jumbles:** DOUBT TYPED SINGLE PURITY
Answer: The only way to learn the coffee business—FROM THE "GROUNDS" UP

132. **Jumbles:** FIFTY GORGE ENDURE ARCTIC
Answer: Retreads are sold for people who want to do this—"RE-TIRE"

133. **Jumbles:** ABOVE BRAIN FELLOW ARTFUL
Answer: When you buy a herd of bison, you can expect to receive this—A BUFFALO "BILL"

134. **Jumbles:** TRIPE CROWN FROSTY PAUNCH
Answer: What they served in that restaurant favored by the karate crowd—"CHOPS"

135. **Jumbles:** MOLDY FEIGN BLAZER NEEDLE
Answer: That friendly neighborhood bank catered to people who were this—"LOAN-LY"

136. **Jumbles:** CAPON TWINE WIZARD MOSQUE
Answer: Why pillows are so expensive—DOWN IS UP

137. **Jumbles:** MOUSE TASTY LEDGER PRIMER
Answer: What they were awarded at the graduation ceremonies at diving school—"DEEP-LOMAS"

138. **Jumbles:** ENJOY PRIME SPLICE THORAX
Answer: Is this the best lubricant for furniture wheels?—"CASTER" OIL

139. **Jumbles:** SIEGE WHOSE BOUGHT POTENT
Answer: The smoothest running thing about that car—HIS TONGUE

140. **Jumbles:** SHOWY AROMA NIPPLE FALLEN
Answer: Another name for chivalry—"MALE" POLISH

141. **Jumbles:** FRUIT TOKEN CACTUS LIZARD
Answer: What's missing from most hot disputes?—COLD FACTS

142. **Jumbles:** CRESS GULLY DENTAL BANNER
Answer: What the dynamiters' annual shindig was—A REAL BLAST

143. **Jumbles:** CHEEK NOBLE BESTOW INVADE
Answer: Another thing that people are always spilling—THE BEANS

144. **Jumbles:** SNACK BOOTY POETIC CARBON
Answer: That husband and wife knew each other like a book—A SCRAP BOOK

145. **Jumbles:** FLUKE AGATE THWART SHOULD
Answer: Something one's in when one's not in anything else—THE ALTOGETHER

146. **Jumbles:** COLIC BRAWL MANAGE ABSORB
Answer: What building that big tunnel must have been—A BIG "BORE"

147. **Jumbles:** JERKY FORGO INWARD ABUSED
Answer: The selfish farmhand had trouble milking the cow, because he had no regard for the feeling of this—"UDDERS" (others)

148. **Jumbles:** ROUSE PLAIT SIPHON ALWAYS
Answer: How to mail an umbrella—BY "PARASOL" POST

149. **Jumbles:** BRINY GAUZE PURPLE DECENT
Answer: The diary is the book where all her secrets are this—"PENNED" UP

150. **Jumbles:** ELEGY HOBBY UPSHOT GUIDED
Answer: What the an did when he saw the anteater—BUGGED OUT

151. **Jumbles:** LADLE PROXY AUBURN CATCHY
Answer: Some sailors who make their living on water seldom do this—TOUCH IT ON LAND

152. **Jumbles:** ONION BERET UNLOCK HANGER
Answer: Her choice of husband showed better taste than this—HER COOKING

153. **Jumbles:** EVOKE DRAWL WEAPON ARTERY
Answer: Her strong will dominated this—HIS WEAK "WON'T"

154. **Jumbles:** ANISE DAISY BELIEF FAMOUS
Answer: Women use perfume because some men are easily this—LED BY THE NOSE

155. **Jumbles:** KNACK LEECH QUENCH BEDBUG
Answer: Patent medicines were seldom what they were this—"QUACKED" UP TO BE

156. **Jumbles:** PATCH NIPPY FROZEN ANYONE
Answer: The weather bureau might sometimes be described as this kind of agency-"NON-PROPHET"

157. **Jumbles:** FLOOD TITLE SUBDUE JANGLE
Answer: How to assure that you don't lose money at the track—JUST DON'T GO

158. **Jumbles:** AWASH FAITH POPLIN SOCKET
Answer: Rich relatives left him a yacht, and ever since he's been talking about this—HIS "KIN SHIP"

159. **Jumbles:** FUNNY BUMPY REBUKE TROPHY
Answer: What happened when nylon stockings were first introduced?—THERE WAS A "RUN" ON THEM

160. **Jumbles:** TANGY PANDA REFUGE UPROAR
Answer: A good hamburger is made from this—THE GROUND UP

161. **Jumbles:** ASTHMA CHUBBY GRISLY AVENUE PELVIS OPENLY
Answer: The encyclopedia salesman was involved in this—A VOLUME BUSINESS

162. **Jumbles:** COHORT DEAFEN FINISH TUMULT UNTRUE PENURY
Answer: Why the cook who nibbled all day got fired—HE ATE INTO THE PROFITS

163. **Jumbles:** GOVERN TAUGHT EIGHTY VOLUME LOCATE ZENITH
Answer: Makes sense only for a photographer—A NEGATIVE THOUGHT

164. **Jumbles:** EXHALE OCCULT EYEFUL NUTRIA KIDNAP RECTOR
Answer: What the baseball fans called for when the beer ran out—A RELIEF "PITCHER"

165. **Jumbles:** DEMISE CANKER IMPUGN ELEVEN DISCUS BUNKER
Answer: A cold night can lead to this—A "BURNING" DESIRE

166. **Jumbles:** SIMILE EXPOSE ABSORB ENTITY GLANCE PLAQUE
Answer: What the zoo provided the grizzlies—BEAR NECESSITIES

167. **Jumbles:** POTTER HOOKED BAZAAR FUMBLE ACCENT FALLEN
Answer: A losing runner wants to get here—OFF THE "BEATEN" PATH

168. **Jumbles:** DEADLY ARCTIC GLOBAL WISDOM DREDGE SOIREE
Answer: What they sent back from the tropical island—"WARMEST" REGARDS

169. **Jumbles:** TOWARD CAUCUS POSTAL APPEAR FILLET MEDLEY
Answer: Easy to enjoy in a hotel's posh quarter's—SUITE DREAMS

170. **Jumbles:** BICKER CACTUS DRAGON APPALL BREACH CAJOLE
Answer: Using a charge card for tuition got her this—COLLEGE CREDIT

171. **Jumbles:** INFANT FACADE CODGER ENCORE BEDECK TOFFEE
Answer: Always given by an orchestra—A "CONCERT-ED" EFFORT

172. **Jumbles:** FICKLE HANDED BUTLER DEMURE FROSTY AFLOAT
Answer: A foul-mouthed parrot can do this to a guest—RUFFLE HIS FEATHERS

173. **Jumbles:** MALADY WALLOP HYMNAL IMPAIR NATURE DAWNED
Answer: The result of tapping your savings account—WITHDRAWAL PAIN

174. **Jumbles:** HERMIT EMPIRE FIGURE CASHEW BRIDLE THIRTY
Answer: What the annual penmanship award ceremony was called—A RIGHT WRITE RITE

175. **Jumbles:** JAGGED FALTER ATTAIN CRAYON PLENTY STIGMA
Answer: Where the model ended up after signing a big contract—SITTING PRETTY

176. **Jumbles:** WEAPON GEYSER REDEEM CIPHER NOODLE VIRTUE
Answer: The herd followed the trail boss because he was—A "STEER-ING" WHEEL

177. **Jumbles:** COWARD CALLOW FORGOT LAYOFF WAITER ALKALI
Answer: Erupts when apes get angry—GORILLA WARFARE

178. **Jumbles:** ENZYME AFFIRM ACTING CANINE BUMPER JAUNTY
Answer: What the movers were good at—CARRYING A TUNE

179. **Jumbles:** STUDIO BENUMB HANGAR MATRON SATIRE ARMADA
Answer: They were seen in Italy's biggest city—ROAMIN' ROMANS

180. **Jumbles:** ENTICE SINFUL MEMBER OBJECT PERSON BLAZER
Answer: Lawyers and judges might have these—"BRIEF" ENCOUNTERS

187

Need More Jumbles®?

Jumble® Books

More than 175 puzzles each!

Cowboy Jumble®
• ISBN: 978-1-62937-355-3

Jammin' Jumble®
• ISBN: 978-1-57243-844-6

Java Jumble®
• ISBN: 978-1-60078-415-6

Jet Set Jumble®
• ISBN: 978-1-60078-353-1

Jolly Jumble®
• ISBN: 978-1-60078-214-5

Jumble® Anniversary
• ISBN: 987-1-62937-734-6

Jumble® Ballet
• ISBN: 978-1-62937-616-5

Jumble® Birthday
• ISBN: 978-1-62937-652-3

Jumble® Celebration
• ISBN: 978-1-60078-134-6

Jumble® Champion
• ISBN: 978-1-62937-870-1

Jumble® Coronation
• ISBN: 978-1-62937-976-0

Jumble® Cuisine
• ISBN: 978-1-62937-735-3

Jumble® Drag Race
• ISBN: 978-1-62937-483-3

Jumble® Ever After
• ISBN: 978-1-62937-785-8

Jumble® Explorer
• ISBN: 978-1-60078-854-3

Jumble® Explosion
• ISBN: 978-1-60078-078-3

Jumble® Fever
• ISBN: 978-1-57243-593-3

Jumble® Galaxy
• ISBN: 978-1-60078-583-2

Jumble® Garden
• ISBN: 978-1-62937-653-0

Jumble® Genius
• ISBN: 978-1-57243-896-5

Jumble® Geography
• ISBN: 978-1-62937-615-8

Jumble® Getaway
• ISBN: 978-1-60078-547-4

Jumble® Gold
• ISBN: 978-1-62937-354-6

Jumble® Health
• ISBN: 978-1-63727-085-1

Jumble® Jackpot
• ISBN: 978-1-57243-897-2

Jumble® Jailbreak
• ISBN: 978-1-62937-002-6

Jumble® Jambalaya
• ISBN: 978-1-60078-294-7

Jumble® Jitterbug
• ISBN: 978-1-60078-584-9

Jumble® Journey
• ISBN: 978-1-62937-549-6

Jumble® Jubilation
• ISBN: 978-1-62937-784-1

Jumble® Jubilee
• ISBN: 978-1-57243-231-4

Jumble® Juggernaut
• ISBN: 978-1-60078-026-4

Jumble® Kingdom
• ISBN: 978-1-62937-079-8

Jumble® Knockout
• ISBN: 978-1-62937-078-1

Jumble® Madness
• ISBN: 978-1-892049-24-7

Jumble® Magic
• ISBN: 978-1-60078-795-9

Jumble® Mania
• ISBN: 978-1-57243-697-8

Jumble® Marathon
• ISBN: 978-1-60078-944-1

Jumble® Masterpiece
• ISBN: 978-1-62937-916-6

Jumble® Neighbor
• ISBN: 978-1-62937-845-9

Jumble® Parachute
• ISBN: 978-1-62937-548-9

Jumble® Party
• ISBN: 978-1-63727-008-0

Jumble® Safari
• ISBN: 978-1-60078-675-4

Jumble® Sensation
• ISBN: 978-1-60078-548-1

Jumble® Skyscraper
• ISBN: 978-1-62937-869-5

Jumble® Symphony
• ISBN: 978-1-62937-131-3

Jumble® Theater
• ISBN: 978-1-62937-484-0

Jumble® Time Machine: 1972
• ISBN: 978-1-63727-082-0

Jumble® Trouble
• ISBN: 978-1-62937-917-3

Jumble® University
• ISBN: 978-1-62937-001-9

Jumble® Unleashed
• ISBN: 978-1-62937-844-2

Jumble® Vacation
• ISBN: 978-1-60078-796-6

Jumble® Wedding
• ISBN: 978-1-62937-307-2

Jumble® Workout
• ISBN: 978-1-60078-943-4

Jump, Jive and Jumble®
• ISBN: 978-1-60078-215-2

Lunar Jumble®
• ISBN: 978-1-60078-853-6

Monster Jumble®
• ISBN: 978-1-62937-213-6

Mystic Jumble®
• ISBN: 978-1-62937-130-6

Rainy Day Jumble®
• ISBN: 978-1-60078-352-4

Royal Jumble®
• ISBN: 978-1-60078-738-6

Sports Jumble®
• ISBN: 978-1-57243-113-3

Summer Fun Jumble®
• ISBN: 978-1-57243-114-0

Touchdown Jumble®
• ISBN: 978-1-62937-212-9

Oversize Jumble® Books

More than 500 puzzles!

Colossal Jumble®
• ISBN: 978-1-57243-490-5

Jumbo Jumble®
• ISBN: 978-1-57243-314-4

Jumble® Crosswords™

More than 175 puzzles!

Jumble® Crosswords™
• ISBN: 978-1-57243-347-2